WE SPOKE IN WHISPERS

By Edward Denmark

Dedicated to my beautiful wife Tricia

Every painful footstep I've taken in my life was worth it to reach you.

Eddy

Front photograph by John Oliver

First published in the UK in 2017 by A. Sykes

8 Tower Road South, Heswall, Wirral, CH60 7SZ

This paperback and digital edition was published in 2017.

As I stood in the congregation on a hot August day in 1979, I looked around at the faces of my family my seven sisters my two brothers and my father. Each one of their faces was etched in sorrow and hurt. My father, never a man to show his emotions, looked lost and bewildered and little wonder this was the funeral of his wife, our mother.

Though hot outside, the church was cool despite the assembled crowd of relative's friends and well-wishers. There were people who I had never seen before, they were complete strangers, and I struggled to understand why they had left it until now to make an effort why now when it was too late? Some of the congregation all dressed in stuffy sombre suits and huge pearls averted my gaze when they caught me looking at them. I wondered if they felt any guilt or embarrassment having only made an effort now.

"Where were you when she needed you?" I thought.

I always knew that we were poor. We lived in a council house, and there were far too many of us, so people never came, until now. I listened as the vicar said polite and kind things about my mother and why all this had happened. Who had given him his information I still don't know, but it didn't sound like the person I knew.

He never mentioned the important things about my mother, yes, she drank too much, and that's why we were all here today. But my mother had qualities that most people were unaware of. She cared for people and most of all us, her family, this was somewhat diminished when she was drunk because sadly the drink masked all her good points. I had been witness to her astute mind as she worked out how she was going to put food on the table before my father returned from work.

Some days it was a close-run thing, and it looked like empty plates but she nearly always managed to pull the rabbit out of the hat at the last minute.

My father would walk in the door asking, "What's for tea?" not knowing that it was nearly fresh air.

The way my mother juggled her debts to rob Peter to pay Paul would have made anyone working on the stock exchange jealous.

The service over we all made our way outside where people were patting each other on the back saying never mind. I stood there feeling very awkward in my black crushed velvet jacket and huge knotted tie that were the fashion of the time.

"What now?" I thought, "Where do I go? What do I say? should I be crying, as some of my sisters still were?"

I had never been to a funeral at all, in fact apart from when our family dog died, I had never had to deal with bereavement before and just didn't know how I was supposed to be feeling. I felt a great sense of loss, yes, but I also wondered how we would all cope now.

My younger sister, Mary, patted me on the back.

"Come on," she urged me, "let's get into the car".

"Where are we going now?" I asked her.

"Home," she answered with a smile.

That night I lay in bed and felt total despair. The day's events played through my mind as the reality began to sink in. I wondered how this would affect all the rest of my family.

I was 18 years old, and I was in a dead-end job at the local chocolate factory I had hardly had what could be described as an education, and furthermore, I didn't know where my life was going. I had always felt very insecure, but lying there in the darkness, I felt so vulnerable and scared. I could no longer hold on, and the pain I felt began to hurt. I sobbed and cried into my pillow. I felt sorry for myself, yes, but I also felt anger at the world, and I also felt jealous of all my friends who had never had to go through this. Why had they been the ones to have the new bike, the new uniform for school, why had their houses always looked posh and not mine? I curled up holding on to my pillow while the tears cascaded down my face and I thought back to my childhood and all the events that had brought me to here, and it all began to fall into place.

Author, aged 7, Moreton Shore

I had spent the best part of a year as a baby in a nearby rehabilitation hospital suffering from some kind of chest illness as a result of being born prematurely at seven months. This hospital treated children with long-term ailments such as tuberculosis etc. When I was due to go home my mother's sister, my Aunty Beatrice volunteered to take me to stay at her house with her and husband Joe and build up my strength until I was strong enough to go home. My aunty, Beatrice, only had a young daughter at the time, Janet, so it was an ideal arrangement. I stayed there for quite a while, and as would happen, my aunt and uncle became very attached to me, and so it must have been heart-breaking for them when my mother decided she wanted me home. By all accounts, they had looked after me well and made me strong. I have no recollection of those days but how kind and loving of them to help me. I was taken back home now, walking, carrying a little suitcase with my clothes and pyjamas inside and holding a teddy bear. My aunty heartbroken had to slip out the door and leave me to my fate. I think had she had known how desperate my life was to become it would have been even harder, but as for me, I was too young to understand that my life had just taken one of many twists that would not be in my favour. As I go on to explain we were a large family and I cannot understand why my parents didn't leave me where I was in safety and comfort where I had at least a good start in life, but that was their decision, and I had no say. I do wonder how different my life would have been though if I had been raised by my aunty.

Author's mother

Ours was a typical three-bedroom council house in Moreton Wirral slap bang in the middle of the peninsula that lies between the River Mersey and the River Dee. These houses can be found on any slightly run-down council estate anywhere. What was different about ours was the number of occupants; there were 12 in total. My two brothers Peter and Boe, and my seven sisters Mary, Ally, Linda, Sue, Irene, Doris and Jean. Jean had moved out early on, to live in South Shields, after meeting her future husband, while serving in the fire brigade. My brother Pete had joined the Merchant Navy, following in the footsteps of my father, who had spent many years at sea, though my father was now serving on the pilot ships, as an engineer. My father worked on the River Mersey and was away for days at a time. I still have vivid memories of going to the landing stage, with my mother, at Birkenhead, to meet him as his ship came in. I felt slightly in awe of him decked out in his uniform and peaked cap as he strode towards us.

Author's father

I recall with fond memories the morning of my first day at school I was smart and proud in my new uniform. My mother fussed around me making sure that I had eaten my breakfast. I felt very grown up. This was it for me, I was one of the big ones, as my mother referred to my older sisters. We sat around a huge table that was pushed into the corner of the living room, as a fire roared in the hearth, life was sweet, and I was very content. Our home was nothing lavish we had linoleum on the floor not carpet and the bedding arrangements were somewhat overcrowded, but everything was spotlessly clean. My mother baked tray after tray of cakes and dished them out to the endless procession of children waiting to be fed. She cared for all of us, and this was reflected in her endless energy to keep us all fed and clothed. I felt the happiness and contentment of a cared-for child. I vividly remember the sweet smell of the cakes and the smell of clean linen as my mother ironed the piles of clothing.

The only cares in the world I had at the time were the daily fights with my sisters. The fights were overall harmless but on occasions they did turn nasty. I once retaliated after a fight at the top of the stairs with one of my sisters by hitting her over the head with my toy rifle as she tried to escape. The rifle was very heavy as it was partly made of die cast metal. It had the desired effect because she let out a high-pitched scream. My mother was up the stairs in the blink of an eye, as I had drawn blood. I received a slap, but as far as I was concerned, I had won.

There was always an ancient washing machine in the kitchen beating the grime out the clothes, before this my mother done it all by hand. There was an old kettle on the cooker, the whistle long gone, and an iron that was heated on the gas!

Little did I know at the time but over the next few years my sweet and content childhood would be drawing to a close and along with my sisters who still lived at home we were about to embark on a nightmare journey into adulthood and the reason? My mother was on a slippery slope of drinking.

I don't know when she finally succumbed to the demon drink, I was too young to notice, but I began to pick up the signs that something was not quite right. My mother's character began to change it was not overnight or anything sudden, but she started to care less and less about the house, and more importantly about our appearance and how we went to school. She still cared and loved us, of that I'm in no doubt, but as the drink began to take hold, she plunged deeper and deeper into debt, and the need for the next drink began to consume all her time and energy. She was always distracted and if we pestered she would get angry that we had interrupted her thoughts. The house never really had much anyway but that little also disappeared and then things like the porridge we had for breakfast in the early days stopped, and we went to school hungry.

Children being children the kids in school were first to pick up on our scruffy appearance. It was very gradual at first but then bullying started with a vengeance, and in my case the chief instigator was a lad called Robert Smith. He was a loathsome character who wanted for nothing, and he was in his element when he had an audience and a victim he could torment, and there were a few of them, only now I was one of them. The teachers either walked around with their eyes closed or chose not to see it I suspect it was the latter. They certainly had their favourites who happened to be the well-dressed kids. The same ones were picked as milk monitors or trusted to run errands to the Headmaster, no matter how long we, the scruffy urchins, held our hands up hoping to be picked it was never to be.

The gap between those who had and those who had not was echoed throughout the school and the playground. When the star players who again happened to be the well-off kids picked the football teams, I was always the last to be picked along with the other scruffs.

"Why do I have to have that tramp in my team?" the unlucky picker who had me would shout.

It had nothing to do with how well I played football. I was dressed like a tramp as far as the other lads were concerned. I would stand alone pretending not to hear, but inside I was devastated and embarrassed.

"You're on our side," the unlucky picker would shout, "so, stay out of the way."

For me, school wasn't a place of happiness or learning, it was a place of misery and bullying that I just had to endure and the fact it was meant to be a place of learning never entered my head. Because of this, I began using and inventing every excuse to avoid going to school. My absences would stretch for weeks and weeks at a time, so, I was effectively not even following the school curriculum. On my return, I would be at a loss to keep up with any projects or assignments. Surprisingly though, I developed a talent for catching on quickly, and I was amused that some of the kids who hadn't had even a single day off would be scratching their heads in confusion and asking me how to solve things.

I was my happiest running around the streets getting into mischief. There were many large families living on the road at this time. One of them, the Cooks, who lived next door, were rather like us, they had nothing. They too had a mixture of boys and girls, so we all had a playmate. In the hot summer months of the school holidays, our street must have resembled a battleground as we went to war with the Cooks after some minor disagreement. Mr Cook had wisely erected a huge fence between the gardens made of scrap wood and old doors, in the hope of separating the feuding mob. Unable to physically get at each other we took to lobbing bricks and stones over the fence. And then we would peep through the cracks to see if we had been victorious in injuring one of the enemies. More often than not a tell-tale scream would indicate a hit before we could even get to look. This stone throwing would go on and on until someone took a hit that was severe enough to send him or her running into the house crying and then the parents would call a halt to the fun.

My mother began to get money from any source available, and in all fairness, my father was not overly generous in the housekeeping department, despite the number of children it was meant to feed. A frequent source of money was the electricity meter, and our family was by no means the only one in the road to use the meter as a private piggy bank. Somebody would be posted by the window, as a lookout, in case my father, who had now taken a job at the local chocolate factory, came strolling down the road or worse still the electric board. On the rare occasions, the meter was emptied 'legitimately', the Electric Man would pile all the foreign coins that had been put into the meter to one side. My mother would look at the assembled kids and ask who put that in there and then she would apologise on our behalf. It was always a happy time when the meter was emptied because this meant we would eat. We would all go into the street laughing as the electricity man banged on the door of one of the families who had raided their meter.

"They're in Mister," we would say, "we have just seen them."

The next time around it could be our turn to hide.

I often wonder even to this day if my father knew that my mother's drinking was spiralling out of control or he kept silent because he spent most of his time in the pub at the end of our road. He would come home from the pub, where he had gone straight from work, pull the table up to his chair, draw the curtains and put the horse-racing on the television and my mother would bring his dinner. Woe betides anybody who dares pass the screen and block his view, even for a second. We had to crawl on hands and knees so as not obscure his view. His tea over, he would make his way back to the pub. He wasn't alone in this way of life many of the men lived like that I wasn't sure if it had something to do with what they had been through in the war.

Moreton was a huge playground in our young eyes with a host of attractions and in particular, the railway that ran past the end of our garden. We were oblivious to the dangers. The railway was the main line that the trains used to take passengers from the Wirral, under the River Mersey, to Liverpool. We viewed it as our own personal train set and any trains passing were fair game. We would get up to all kinds of mischief on the railway, and considering it was an electrified track, I'm amazed none of us were killed on it.

Our favourite past time was pulling the springs from old mattresses that lay around and throwing them onto the live rail. This would cause a big explosion as the wire made contact and we would all scarper. We would cross the railway without thought for our safety, as we made our way to some of the other attractions in the area, like the brickworks at the back of our house or the massive clay quarry, that served the brickworks. Though these places were dangerous to us young tearaways, they were just playgrounds, somewhere to have some fun.

I was more often than not accompanied by our family dog, Bob, on my adventures to the quarry or brickworks. This wasn't out of any loyalty from the dog, it's just that he had worked out if he followed me he was in for a good time chasing rats and rolling in the mud. The downside to this was after the dog had got fed up he would make his own way home caked in mud and whatever else he had rolled in and then go upstairs and lie on the bed for a snooze. The end result was I got a good smack on my return home. I along with my mates tried all kinds of ingenious ways of losing him, including, leaving him in phone boxes, but when we arrived at the quarry, he would already be there tail wagging.

Moreton Brickworks, our playground

The quarry provided hours and hours of fun we would slide down the big dusty face on old boards taken from washing machines and make rafts to sail over the rain filled pit. At that time, I could not swim an inch, but I gave no thought to the consequences had I fallen into the water. I recall one hot summer day, after going down the dusty slide for the umpteen time, feeling a draft. On inspecting my shorts which also served as my school pants I was horrified to find the cheeks of my arse hanging out, I had worn a hole in my pants. On returning home, I was subjected to a barrage of abuse and told to mend them myself, and I did with the only thing I could find white cotton. I put huge dog-stitches in and pulled the holes together crudely' unwittingly I had supplied the loathsome Robert Smith with something more to bully me with.

Our road was always a hive of activity with gangs of kids running up and down all playing in groups. These groups were defined by certain rules, age, toughness, and what part of the street you lived in. Sometimes groups would turn on each other, over minor disagreements, and then life would be difficult if you had to pass through the enemy's location. To avoid this, you would make great detours, and it was tiring and time-consuming. So, when my mother or father wanted something from the shop, they would moan and tell you off for taking so long not knowing what you had done to get them their cigarettes or milk. There were also packs of feral dogs roaming around in those days fighting and humping each other. I watched one day as a dog and a bitch were locked together howling. I thought they were fighting and couldn't understand why the other was on the other ones back. I was stood for ages holding a loaf of bread, and I told a woman who was going past that the two dogs were fighting. She started laughing, and I thought how cruel she was, being happy at them fighting.

My mother's drinking had taken full control of her life and ours by now, and yet no one said a word, in fact, I think some of the older members of my family who had left home had no idea how bad it had become. My parents would return from the pub with my older brother Pete if he was home and his mates all loaded with beer and a card school would begin. The living room would be thick with cigarette smoke, and beer fumes as the drunks hurled profanities at each other. We would stand around waiting to see if they needed anything that, so we might get tipped. I would watch in awe my eyes stinging from the thick, acrid cigarette smoke as these men piled loads of coins onto the table as they lost, they would fart and belch and hurl profanity at each other. This went on all afternoon until the pub opened again and they would all get up and disappear through the door back for more beer. After they had left there would be ashtrays so full the contents had spilt on the floor, so they had taken to putting cigarettes out in empty beer bottles cups and even subbing them out on the table. The toilet upstairs would be overflowing with dark brown urine, and again the ubiquitous cigarette ends. Some would even clear their lungs of phlegm in the sink leaving the luminous green deposits where they landed. I would look at these alien blobs wondering why these men all had this stuff in them. The drunken band of gamblers gone quiet would once again descend on the house. We would carry out a search for any dropped pennies but most it proved fruitless, and we would move on to some other source of thievery.

A pattern began to emerge, and my mother started to get into more and more debt, and I found it hard to understand her moods at the time. She would send us around to the neighbours asking if they could lend her some money. My sisters and I had the speech off pat.

"Me mum said could you possibly lend her a pound until she gets paid on Thursday she wouldn't ask, but she's desperate."

Mostly the people genuinely didn't have the money to borrow. If we failed at one house, we would be sent to the next. If we were successful, my mother's mood would change to joy. We can get some food now she would say putting on her coat. Our house though never lavishly furnished was also beginning to look worse for wear and dirty and again this was picked up by the other kids in the street who themselves had nothing, but their houses were clean. Even the essentials for cleanliness like toothbrushes, toothpaste and soap, were no longer being bought, so our hygiene undoubtedly began to decline. My mother also got into a routine of sending us down to the local pub of an evening to get whiskey for her. My father would be propped up at the bar or playing darts, and we would look through a small clear gap in the frosted windows trying to attract his attention. What does she want he would say when he eventually came to the door?

And once again we would reel off a well-rehearsed speech, "Me mum said can you get her a quarter bottle of whiskey and if not a miniature bottle and she will give you the money on Thursday."

My father would then come out with his well-rehearsed speech, "I'm sick of this I haven't got any money," but then he would go and get it.

It always baffled me even at this young age. Why did my father always say that he didn't have any money? He must have money if he was in the pub. On the occasions, my father refused to get the whiskey again on the pretence he had no money, and we returned home empty-handed my mother would erupt in a fury.

"The lousy bastard!" she would scream hurling abuse at no one in particular.

Then her anger would be dished out to all present, "You can all fuck off!" she would scream, "Because from now on I will look after myself. Sod the lot of you."

This would go on until she had vented her anger.

I hated this part of my life as much as a hated the bullying in school and I think I resented my mother as much as the bullies; in my mind, they were all making my life a misery. My sisters and I accepted our lot because we had no option, what else could we do? This was as good as it gets. Yes, I dreamed of running away, but I knew that's all it was a dream' on the other hand my dream of leaving home once I had left school was reality and it was something that kept me going during the very worst times. I looked on the years ahead as a prison sentence, and I would be overjoyed as one year gave way to the next knowing that I would be able to leave without looking back.

No one and nothing escaped my mother's scams to get money she was as cunning as a fox, but sometimes people left themselves wide open and came to the house like lambs to the slaughter. One day a booted and suited salesman knocked on our door and asked one of the scruffy urchins who opened it if my mother was in.

"No," came the reply as we had all been taught in case the visitor was after money, but my mother appeared at the door a second later after seeing this particular guest was bearing gifts.

"Take no notice," she said, "The kids are always fooling around, can I help you?"

It turned out that the salesman was working for some enterprising company who were renting out cigarette machines. The idea was the recipient would keep the device in the house. Instead of going out to the shops for the cigarettes they could simply purchase them from the machine, as could any guests to the house but the prices were loaded so the company could make a tidy profit. The salesman was obviously new to the job or simply didn't see that he was never going make any money from this house in a million years if he had bothered to look closely he would have seen that we didn't have two pennies to rub together.

He came into the house and gave my mother a full demonstration of the machine, putting his own money into it and tossing a packet of cigarettes to my mother.

"They're yours, on the house," he said, with a smile.

This was no doubt part of the marketing strategy.

"Oh, thanks very, much," my mother replied.

All the paperwork filled in the salesman pulled out his little tool bag and promptly looked around for the best place to bolt the cigarette machine to a wall. He looked at the wall near my mother's chair, and the remains of about two thousand blue bottle flies squashed on the wall in various states of decay and in some cases so old they had actually mummified.

"I tell you what," he said, "let's put it in the hallway".

"Okay," my mother agreed, "good idea".

The hall wasn't too much better, but he found an unoccupied patch and bolted the machine to the wall and said his farewells promising to return each week to fill the machine with cigarettes and empty the cash drawer.

"Goodbye, then," he said with a smug look on his face having just secured a sale from the peasants.

The salesman hadn't cleared the path before my mother was on the machine prising open the draws open with a screwdriver and emptying the cigarettes out. The device was tossed into the corner testimony to yet another failed venture. The salesman persisted for a few months before giving up. He received neither any of the cigarettes or a single penny.

One warm summer's day our dog, Bob, involuntarily emptied his bowels and was rushed to the vets. The vet decided that this mangy old mutt had, had his day and he was put down I was devastated. It was my first experience of bereavement, and I cried my eyes out all day. No more dogs my dad insisted that's the end of it. The positive side to Bob's departure was that he could no longer betray my excursions to the quarry or the brickworks.

Lingham School, the place of so much misery

One day, a trip out, nearly ended in me being hurt. Along with a few of the lads from the street, we decided to go and play with the cables that the carts ran along bringing the clay from the quarry. They were about 10 feet off the ground, but we soon realised that if a couple of the lads climbed up the supporting arm, their combined weight would bring the cable down within reach of the rest of us. The idea then was we would all hold on to the cable then a few would let go, and the rest of us would be catapulted up into the air letting go at just a couple of feet of the ground. Either I mistimed it, or I failed to understand the instructions, but I found myself flying well above the height of two feet. To everyone's amusement, I came crashing down into puddle on my arse and even before I had hit the ground I was crying in anticipation of the pain that would surely come. I was not disappointed I felt like my arse had come through my neck when I landed.

The old bridge across to Moreton Quarry

Sometime after this episode, I was again, hanging about the prefab housing because they had been mostly emptied out ready for demolition, but there were still one or two residents still there. Most of the ones who had moved had left the curtains up as they had small windows and were unlikely to fit anywhere else. Walking around with a lad from my road one day we started looking in the abandoned houses to see if there was anything we could smash or steal. We were having a jolly time smashing windows and generally causing mayhem. After coming out of umpteen houses, we wandered along to another house.

The lad I was with said, "Let's go in this one," pointing at yet another prefab.

I was about to say to him and bit my lip.

"No," I said, "better still I bet you can't put the window in from here with a brick?"

"Watch," he said and with that picked a half-brick up and threw it with the skill of a professional cricketer at the window in the living room.

The sound as the glass smashed and cascaded all over the lawn was deafening. In an instant, the front door opened and a woman stood screaming obscenities. I began to run, and the lad followed me but he was crying, tears streaming down his face. I had tears streaming down my face, but they were not tears of fear I was laughing because I knew someone was still living there. We ran and ran until we got to our road and hid in our garden. The lad was panic stricken.

"What if the police come," he was saying, "I'm going get sent to prison."

"You won't," I soothed him, "she doesn't know who you are does she?"

He calmed down a little at this, so I added, "but she knows me!"

He burst out crying again.

"No, she doesn't," I teased playing with his emotions, "I'm only joking."

He was so worried he made me rehearse that it wasn't us who did it in the event the police would turn up. Nothing ever came of it, but I never told him that I knew the house was occupied.

Our home life was still dominated by lack of cash and too much alcohol. My mother's financial escapades continued, and in all honesty, she must have had a great mind to dream up some of her scams to get money, but occasionally, she was caught out. After receiving a few items from a credit company, namely our Christmas presents, she once again forgot to pay for them. This particular group were more ruthless than most, and about a month after Christmas, they turned up at our houses demanding payment for the two prams my mother had got for my sisters Mary and Ally.

"I haven't got any money," she argued, as Mary and Ally, who were blissfully unaware, pushed their prams proudly down the road.

The eagle-eyed debt collector turned on his heels marched up to my sisters and took the prams of them, after emptying their dolls out, and put them into his car. He looked over at me, as I stood open mouthed with my boxing gloves on which I had got for Christmas.

"If they belong to us, I will be back," he said to me.

He drove off up the road followed by abuse and threats; the promised replacements never materialised. And so, life went from one disappointment to the next, but I think by now we were getting used to it and becoming more and more resourceful.

Near to our house, there was a Sunday school, and someone in the school came up with the idea of giving sweets out at the door to encourage the local kids to turn up. A brilliant idea in theory but we the local scoundrels were quick in finding a way of cheating the system without the need to attend. A Sunday school teacher stood on the door and as you went in you were handed a toffee arrow bar and told to sit down, but we simply slipped through a side door and re-joined the queue.

"Weren't you just here?" the teacher would enquire.

"No, that was our kid," we would answer and be given second helpings but inevitably greed would be our downfall, and we would be caught on the third attempt.

Along with my mate, Mick, I became a firm friend with yet another Mick, who had moved into a house next door but one to me. Mick Price, had moved from another area and he was more adventurous than us. I sensed straight away that he was prepared to take a risk, and I was happy because we lacked someone like this. Mick Price had two other brothers, John, who was older and Billy, who was younger and, a sister, Chris. His mum and dad, John and Phyllis, were good people.

In much later years when I had a brief stint out the army, I joined the Royal Marines Reserve, and I also convinced Mick Price to join, as I knew he had the ability to become a commando. Mick and I would run and train and go to Cumbria climbing and camping. He went on to gain his coveted green beret.

He was also a very skilled builder and carpenter. At the time, during our long talks about the military, Mick would ask me about the Falklands War and Northern Ireland. He was really interested and would ask questions about every little detail, and I would spill my heart out. It would sometimes feel very emotional as he probed me for more information. I would then remember things from the back of my mind, where they had been pushed by my subconscious, unable to deal with them, but Mick would coax them out. At the time I didn't realise it, but Mick, was in his own way, whether he knew it or not, counselling me, as far as my mental health problems concerning battle shock were concerned.

Also, next door to us the Cooks had upped sticks and left. A more sedate family, called the Lambirds, had moved in and with them

Trevor, who was the same age as me, but he was more reserved and quiet. However, he did have some nice sisters, Gilly, who was my age, Susan and Carol, who were both stunners but too old for me.

Life during school hours was becoming increasingly miserable as the bullying continued and this was not helped by the fact most of the other lads were now wearing long trousers, and I still had shorts. The reason for this was that the shorts we were marginally cheaper to buy, so, that's what I got. My protests and pleading to my parents fell on deaf ears. I watched as my mother drank her usual bottle of whiskey and my dad continued to throw his money across the bar down at the local pub knowing that the money could have bought me a pair of long trousers and eased some of my misery. I despised him and her for their selfishness. I pleaded with my father for a long pair of pants, even trying to convince him that they would last me much longer than shorts but like my mother, he wasn't interested, and that night he was in the pub spending his money.

I possessed neither a toothbrush or even a change of clothes. I didn't even have a wardrobe or drawer, where I could go for a change of clothes. I would simply go to a large cupboard in our kitchen and trawl through the dirty washing and drag something out to wear. Once, I got out of bed one morning and put on my socks that I had worn continually for months on end, they simply fell apart. With no exaggeration, the socks had become brittle and hard through months of dirt and sweat. I permanently had dirt under my fingernails, which were left unclipped. My hair was akin to a Guardsman's bearskin hat. I must have looked like a caveman as wandered the streets.

Author on Holy Island, aged 12

Author, again, on Holy Island

This was certainly the point where our appearance had taken a turn for the worse. I recall with horrifying clarity going to school one day with the sole hanging off my shoe, and as I walked it would slap the ground, I must have sounded like a horse. Even worse when I realised that I was late for school I began to run. The sole started making a noise like a machine gun, and everyone looked at me with astonishment. As I turned the corner and the school was in sight, the sole made one last slap on the ground, and it parted company from the rest of my shoe exposing my socks which were made up of more holes than sock revealing my black, unwashed toes. I walked back home petrified. I left the upper part of my shoe hanging around my ankle hoping nobody would notice. I was taken to Birkenhead market the following day, and my mother brought me a pair off the second-hand stall. I was elated.

The day before returning to school after the summer holidays I was convinced that my mother had finally come to understand my embarrassment at having to wear shorts for school. She came back from a shopping trip with a brown bag.

"I've got you something smart for you to go back to school in," she said with a smile on her face.

I could feel the emotion rise in my stomach as I thought of being able to hold my head high, that is until she pulled the contents of the bag out. A pair of dark checked shorts complete with matching jacket, both looked like something worn by children during the war. I was horrified I could not believe that anybody could be so cruel and if I'm honest, I hated my mother at that moment. I knew if I was to protest it would be futile so I silently tried the suit on as ordered and placing my hands in the pocket I discovered crumbs and sweet wrappers it was second hand. That night I lay in bed crying, and I sobbed myself to sleep knowing the bullies would have a good laugh at my expense, and my own mother had given them the ammunition. Robert Smith and his cronies were delighted when I turned up looking like a clown even the teacher sniggered.

I wonder to this day how we as children were not abducted or killed living the life we led. It was chaotic and without order or restraint. No one had any idea where we were or what we were up to. My mum and dad seemed to live separate lives, as far running the house was concerned. My dad gave my mum money and not enough, and she was left to do everything but was now incapable of doing it. Her health was not good due to her alcohol intake, and she had all but given up. But still, my dad carried on with his life and his routine which on reflection was rather odd, indifferent, uncaring. I don't know, but he never changed his ways and as far as I am aware, made no intervention to stop what was happening or get her some help. He paid no attention to us and never engaged us in conversation or offered us any advice or encouragement. I would go as far as to say I didn't even really know him.

He was a person of routine, and he never changed from that routine in any way. I never once recall him missing his pint of beer in the pub or staying off work through illness. He never once visited a doctor ever until he reached old age. I don't recall him ever wishing me happy birthday or offering to take us out to the beach, in fact, I never once saw my dad go to the beach even though it was no more than a half a mile away.

Sometimes he would bring home the seconds chocolate bars from Cadbury's which could not be sold in the shops. He would bring back Skippy bars and Bar Six which we all loved, but that was it. That really was the extent of his parental duties. We had aunties and uncles who would pop in from time, to time but I never took much notice of them, so I didn't know if they knew of the situation. I am sure some of my mum's friends knew, but I don't think they really knew the truth. I certainly tried to keep it from my friends but they did ask questions, and I knew they wondered why the house was so scruffy given my father worked and not only that he was in a very good job and earned good money. He was never ever, in the position of having no money, EVER and yet he was surrounded by such desperate poverty and hungry children. It seems incredible that a man could sit with money in his pocket knowing that his family and young children had nothing to eat and were living in such squalor.

Yes, my mum was always buying alcohol because as an alcoholic, with such an illness, and addiction, that had hold of her she couldn't beat it, not for her sake not for even our sake. But nothing was stopping him from taking control or buying the food himself and even making sure we had shoes. He watched us trudge to school on the occasions we went in the bitter winter wearing nothing but school pumps with holes in them. I would sit in the class with an empty stomach and wet, freezing cold feet, listening to Robert Smith calling me names. It was hardly the best environment to learn, but it was my lot, and amazingly I never felt sorry for myself I just accepted that it was how life was.

The only thing that kept me upright during those hard days in class was the free bottle of milk that each child was given, and I can tell you never were it needed more. Years later, when I was shaking hands with the then Prime Minister, Margaret Thatcher, I should have told her that her decision to take this free milk away was a terrible mistake. It could be that my dad had a hard, early life himself I don't know, but I made sure that my children were looked after and given a decent life.

I wasn't unique in my plight I don't think because there were certainly one or two other kids who looked no better off than me in the wardrobe department. I did wonder what their stories were. Did they have a parent who drank or did they simply have no money? Strangely these other children gave me some comfort to see that there were others who had it hard as well as me so if they could cope so could I. Yet despite our shared bond of misery we, scruffy bunch of outsiders, didn't gel together for comfort.

It wasn't just us either anyone who had anything that was outside the realms of what was considered normal was fair game to the bullies.

Not wishing to stereotype anyone but there was always a child with a big shoe, that was extended on the sole, to give height because of one short leg. A few kids wore callipers, which were a metal contraption, worn on the leg, because of a foot misaligning, or as it was referred to, before the invention of political correctness, 'A club foot'. There were one or two obese children who were teased and called 'Fatty' and then a sprinkling of children who wore national health issue glasses, with an eye patch, to treat a lazy eye. In the playground, the great unwashed would all walk around while the 'normal kids' played football or war. I became very adept at spotting a crisp on the playground floor dropped by someone who didn't have a rumbling tummy like me. I would walk over and pretend to sit by it and then get it and walk away and eat it without being seen.

My biggest challenge was hunger most days, and I was always on the look out to solve it, but just sometimes it was taken care of without effort, and on one such day we were taken out on a day trip to Wales which to us was the other side of the world.

The trip was out of the blue and organised by a women's charity of one sort or another. I never even found out how it came about, all I was interested in was that I was going on a big adventure with my sisters and few of the other kids out of the road. It was an old coach, and I recall with utter excitement as we climbed on board full of anticipation. We were given the warning to behave ourselves and any last toilet requests. I was nearly peeing myself with excitement! We all chatted looking out the windows as the coach pulled away. 10 minutes into the journey one of the elderly women came around and handed us a carton of orange juice. I was so grateful it was a hot sunny day, and air conditioning in coaches was a long way off.

As we left the Wirral and made our way towards Betws-y-Coed, North Wales, we looked on in fascination at the sheep and hills. It wasn't long before the first toilet stop. Excited children and small bladders are a bad mix. I really thought I had travelled to another world, I had no real idea of where I was apart from Wales, but it was the adventure I loved. We arrived in Betws-y-Coed and were herded into smaller groups. We started off on a walk, and they took us up a steep hill of long grass and sheep with small rivers. We ran about free, screaming, laughing and rolling down the hills full of joy.

"Be careful," warned the women as we jumped and shouted and ran until our lungs burst.

Cows and sheep looked on puzzled at all the little ruffians hollering and laughing. A local farmer watched us laughing at us. I didn't have a care in the world, I had forgotten my plight, I had forgotten Robert Smith and even though I was hungry, that was now out of my thoughts. The muscles in my legs burnt as I chased my sisters up the hill and sweat rolled off me.

"Right children," shouted one of the women gather up.

The fun is over I thought ready to get back on the coach.

"Okay," said the Lady in charge of our little group, "we are now going to walk back towards the coach and go and have lunch."

"Lunch?" I thought what is she on about, I haven't got any food with me and as far as I know, my sister hadn't either.

I sidled up to the woman and tugged at her skirt "Miss, Miss," I whispered.

The kind lady looked down at me.

"What is it?" She asked me.

"I don't have any food with me. I forgot it," I lied.

The lady laughed.

"Oh, don't worry," she replied, "we have food for you, now run along."

They have food, this really was turning out to be a really, really good day. We all walked along the road and stopped at a large wooden hut.

"Right!" someone shouted, "Go in, in an orderly fashion and take a seat."

We all trooped in, and I caught sight of table after table groaning under the weight of food! I couldn't believe it, I had never seen such A vast amount, and there were sandwiches, sausage rolls, pies even cakes and large jugs of orange juice. We each had a bar of rock next to our plates.

"Don't touch the food yet," we were told.

Once we were all seated. The lady next to me said, "Okay children, begin".

And so, I started eating and eating. After a half hour, I could eat no more, and my stomach was bursting to the point I felt ill. After everyone had finished, we were told to go outside ready for a last walk before heading back. I had eaten that much I couldn't walk and began crying. The lady understood my plight and led me to a chair.

"You sit there, dear" she soothed, "let your lunch go down while the other children go for a walk."

I sat there for about two hours and even then, could only manage to walk back to the coach. I still had a tight hold on my bar of rock though because I knew this strange feeling of being full was only temporary.

Disappointment was a way of life in our family, and we had come to expect it, but sometimes we were still gullible to the promises made by my mother. Chopper bikes were all the rage when I was a child, and I would look on with a burning jealousy as the same kids who got everything in our road flaunted their bikes. And so, I was delighted when my mother presented me with a card showing she had made a deposit on a chopper bike. It was only the first payment, and there would have to be another thirty or so, but it was a start. I studied the little yellow payment card for hours reading the words chopper bike over and over again. But alas true to form only one payment was ever made and that was retrieved later that week' it was after all only a dream, and in my heart, I knew it.

The new lad in the road, Mick Price, was as I had thought more adventurous than the rest of us and with his influence we started looking further afield for our entertainment. We still hung around the brickworks and the quarry, but he showed us how to bunk onto the train from our home station to Liverpool. We would descend on to Lewis's one of Liverpool's high-class department stores much to the dismay of the staff who really did look down their noses at the scruffy band of children.

The lowest priced meal in the restaurant was chips and beans at 25p. This was the only meal within our price budget, and even this was only possible if we had managed to evade paying our fare on the train. The snooty women behind the counter would first ask to see our money before they would dish the food out. Once the food had been eaten with the finesse of a starving dog, we would then set about some real mischief within the various departments in the store until the staff grew tired and chased us.

On my arrival home from these adventures, I was rarely questioned as to where I had been' which suited me fine. But because of this loose rein, I was on a slippery slope, and it wasn't long before I had my first brush with the law. After returning to the Wirral from Liverpool by train with Mick and two other lads from our road. We spotted two girls who lived near us, they were in the waiting room on the station. We decided to play a prank on them by holding the door on the waiting room when their train arrived in the station. It really was only a joke, and it certainly wasn't meant to be malicious because we were going to let them out at the last minute.

Mick and I held the door while the other two lads laughed as the girls banged furiously on the door pleading to be realised. Even some of the passengers who were on the train were laughing. In a split second, the joke took a sinister turn as one of the girls banged a little too hard on the glass and it shattered cutting her hand. The sight of blood threw us into sheer panic, and we ran fast, I knew we had gone too far, we were in serious trouble.

We ran to the sanctuary of the nearest church where we could decide what to do. We were in trouble of that we were sure. After much debate, we decided on the direct approach knock on the girl's door and apologise in the vain hope that we could keep it from our parents. This was a bad move. The girl's older sister opened the door, and in between her torrents of abuse, she told us the police had been informed, and they were probably waiting for us at home.

We walked back in silence our fate had been sealed. The girl's sister was right the police were waiting. A few weeks later we all appeared in court, and each of us was fined less than one pound. Only two of the lads with us, Stewart Martindale, and his brother, Gordon, put up a fight by, rightly, saying it was an accident nothing more but their plea fell on deaf ears, and they paid up just like us. The girl did not bear any grudges because I began dating her shortly afterwards. I think she understood, better than her older sister, that there was no malice intended, it was just a joke that went wrong.

Whenever I called around to my friend's houses, I couldn't help but notice that their homes were much nicer than my own much nicer I know now because they were normal, clean and tidy. I did feel embarrassed if my friends knocked for me. I even began to invent stories saying that we were about to decorate. But after a couple of years my mates saw through it, and when we fell out as young children inevitably do, they would let it all out calling me a tramp and say that my home was a dump.

So, this was it, my childhood was all mapped out and drink would be the captain in deciding which direction it should go. In my naivety, I thought that maybe my mother would give up the drink and everything would be okay. It was not to be, and I soon learned to live on my wit and take each day at a time.

I wonder even today why the authorities did not pick up on our scruffy appearance and continuous absence from school. After all, this was not some back-street tenement of the Victorian era it was Merseyside of the late 1960s early 70s. But even I could not have guessed at what lay ahead for me.

The summer months of my younger years seemed to go on forever; certainly, they seemed much hotter. The summer holidays went on for a lifetime. We as children would be packed off to the beach with egg butties and a bottle of lemonade, which never seemed to go around all of us. We would be allowed a cap full each, just enough to wet our mouths. And after spending hours running around under the glare of a furious sun, it was like torture.

We would stop at a small shop on our way to the beach were my older sisters would buy the lemonade. I can recall with clarity to this day being tempted by all the sweets and goodies on offer under my nose. While the shop assistant was busy, I reached over the counter and helped myself to a bar of chocolate. My timing wasn't perfect because she turned around just in time to catch a glimpse of me bringing my arm back over the counter. As I was new to this stealing business, I did not try to hide the evidence or make up an excuse.

I just looked at her with pleading in my eye. The girl must have known I would be for the high jump off my sisters and she said nothing. I hid the chocolate and later disposed of it, as I was too afraid to eat it. Ironically by saying nothing, the girl had taught me a lesson because I knew she had seen me, and that made me feel even worse.

Equally, the winter was much colder in my younger years and snow was guaranteed. The piercing scream of whoever had risen first would wake all in our house.

"It's snowed," would be the cry and we would all hurry to get dressed and play out.

When it had snowed, I would feel elated, in some ways comforted, and I would look forward to school. I have come to realise in later years that this was because the snow was a distraction, a distraction for me and a distraction for the bullies. Why torment the tramp while the snow is here? They could always return to me when it had melted.

During school hours, I come to realise that the best policy was to keep quiet and try and stay out of sight, don't attract any attention and it sometimes paid off. However once or twice it failed, and on one day I was sitting in class when the door swung open, and another teacher came into the class.

The two teachers began having a whispered conversation, and then they both turned looking at me. I started to panic, and I could feel my face redden as all the other children began to turn in their seats as well.

"Edward Denmark, stand up," ordered my teacher.

I stood up silently praying to myself that the earth would open up and swallow me. My mind raced wondering what I had done. I thought over a million excuses, for a few things, that I had possibly been found out for.

Finally, my own teacher spoke up, "Edward, your mother, has been on the telephone to the school asking if you have seen her false teeth."

My heart nearly came out of my chest when the enormity of what I had done hit home. I didn't know which was worse the embarrassment of being found out in front of the class or the consequences of what I had done.

"I swapped them for a fire engine, Miss," I blurted out.

The teachers could not hide their amusement, and my classmates began to snigger.

"You have swapped them for a fire engine," my teacher repeated hardly believing her ears. "Who with?" she asked.

"Terry, Miss", I replied.

"Come with me," the other teacher said to me.

I followed her out of the class. We walked down the corridor to Terry Comber's class.

"Terry, what have you done with the teeth Edward gave you for your fire engine," the teacher asked Terry, who sat there shocked.

He reluctantly pulled the teeth from his grubby pocket and handed them to the teacher.

"What about me fire engine," he asked worriedly thinking I had pulled a stunt on him.

I had the wrath of my mother to face on my return home, but for the rest of the day, I was subjected to horrendous piss taking. It transpired that Terry had been passing the teeth around the school playground letting all the kids have a go. I decided to keep this to myself.

I had a passion for toy cars like any young boy, but I loved nothing more than setting fire to them in the garden. But after a while, the garden became unsafe because of the unwanted attention of my sisters, Mary and Ally, who lost no time in telling on me. So, in my wisdom, I decided to hide in the shed where I carried out my destruction without any interruptions. The shed was full of old rubbish, and hardly anyone used it, so it was perfect for me, or so I thought.

Toy car and pilfered matches in pocket I sneaked into the shed one quiet afternoon. After going through the childish scenario of pretending the car had crashed and all aboard had died of horrific injuries, I struck the match and set the car alight. I watched with the fascination fire has on children as the car burnt. Because this model had lots of plastic extras on it wasn't long before thick black smoke began billowing up around me. Panicking a little I tried blowing the flames out, and in doing so, I was inhaling lungs full of the smoke. I stood up feeling very dizzy and staggered out of the shed and into the house. I made for the stairs hoping that I would have time to recover. But as I made my way up the stairs my elder brother, Pete, was on his way down. He knew instantly that I had been up to no good because I was feeling so light headed that I nearly fell back down. He managed to grab me and so scared was I that confessed what I had been up to.

My brother told my sister, Linda, to phone for an ambulance, which she did, but also telling them that I had set fire to a car. Within minutes the road was full of fire engines, the firemen thought that I had set fire to the real thing. Luckily for me, they were laughing at the mix-up, but I was in deep trouble.

A regular visitor to our house was the local midwife who had practically delivered most of us. The midwife was an enormous, portly woman and I think her visits, which continued long after we had grown beyond infancy, were because she had a genuine interest in our welfare. But because of her size, we would lie on the living room floor and burst into tears with laughter when we had managed a glimpse up her dress at her ample thighs. She knew what the game was, and she would chastise us, but we would always deny it.

Whenever the midwife used the toilet, nobody heard her flush it afterwards, and my brother said she was peeing into the bath because she was too big to sit on the toilet. To confirm this plot was hatched in time for the midwife's next visit. My brother would hide in the loft and watch to see if she really was peeing into the bath. The following week with the precision of a Swiss clock the midwife turned up, and we children could hardly contain our delight at the thought of my brother secreted away in the loft.

To help move things along at a quicker pace, we began plying the midwife with endless cups of tea.

"Oh, you're being extra kind today," she exclaimed with a huge grin.

Eventually, the midwife heaved her large frame from the settee, with a grunt.

"Nature's calls," she said with a smile.

We all rolled about on the floor laughing.

"Shut up," my mother said, scolding us, "it is not that funny," puzzled at our over the top hysterics.

The midwife came back down the stairs and began saying her farewells without even sitting back down, which was what she always did. Before the door had even closed on her, we all rushed up the stairs and into the bathroom just in time to find my brother lowering himself out of the loft.

"Did she pee in the bath?" we all asked laughing, but my brother was laughing so much he could only nod a reply of yes.

After all the laughing had died down my brother gave us all the finer details. It transpired that the midwife had lowered herself over the bath began peeing and then turned the tap on to flush away the evidence. At this point, my brother could only stifle his laughter by forcing his hand into his mouth.

In between these episodes of happy mischief, my life as a whole and that of my sisters had descended into the abyss of poverty and the perpetual misery that is unique to the children of an alcoholic parent. In some ways, I think it would have been easier if it was my father who was the alcoholic, he drank too much and didn't care enough, but he was not an alcoholic as my mother was.

My sisters and I became very familiar with the endless bottles of whiskey my mother would get through. We also became very aware of her moods and temperament in so much as the before and after she had consumed the best part of a bottle of scotch.

Children are by nature very perceptive. If we came home from school on the rare occasions, we attended, and she was asleep in the chair we spoke in whispers to avoid waking her from her drunken stupor, as she would normally be in bad mood as the effects of alcohol wore off. Yet this contrasted with her real nature of being very caring witty and intelligent.

We would get glimpses of the old mother the real person who we all loved when she was at the stage of having just had a drink and therefore not suffer the craving for one and not having had too much. This moment of happiness was only ever short lived because once the drink began to take effect, her personality was gone, she was once more a drunk. But for all that this small window gave us all strength; it reminded us all that there was real person inside this alcoholic.

For me personally, I really despised this dark inoffensive looking liquid that had so much effect on all our lives. I didn't at that time know that alcohol abuse will ultimately kill the abuser, and it was just as well because I had enough emotional trauma to cope with.

Things were undoubtedly becoming more and more desperate for me both at home and at school. My appearance and that of my sisters had become more than scruffy we were down right filthy in our appearance. I began dreading going to school and so I would try all kinds of tricks to avoid it like coughing in the night so my mother would hear me and tell me I could stay off. My sisters were also on to this ploy so most of the time we would all be off school hanging around the house or running messages as my mother called our trips to the neighbours to borrow money. In reality, we were taking advantage of my mother's good nature by pretending to be ill, but it was better than being in school. After the inevitable visit from the school board, we would all be sent back to school the following day with hasty notes scribbled on the back of empty cigarette packets explaining our absence.

The teachers were indifferent as to whether we attended or not. But after putting a full week in we would once again fall into the vicious circle of not attending.

As the advance of home luxuries, like phones and colour televisions, began to appear in my mate's houses, I looked on in jealousy knowing that it would be a long time before these things appeared in our house. It was just another wedge that separated me and left me out when they would talk about watching programs in colour, and I could add nothing. There really was no hope because we still had to eat our dinner out of pan lids because there weren't enough plates to go around and what plates there were the older children got first. I can still recall holding my finger over the little round steam vent in the lid to stop the gravy running out.

School and education were still not a priority for me or indeed my mother because I only went when it was absolutely necessary. I reasoned in my young mind that whatever they wanted to teach me didn't matter because I would get a job somewhere. I didn't have the foresight to think that education would determine what kind job I got would depend on my level of education. To me, all the hassle of putting up with the likes of Robert Smith were simply not worth the trouble, so it was easier not seeing him.

Sometimes, however, luck was not on my side and on one particular day as we were being led from the playground into the school in a long line, I stood in dog shit! I was in a dilemma as to whether I should drop out the line and clean my shoe and suffer the horrendous piss taking or what? So, I just carried on as if nothing had happened and arrived in class. I desperately tried to clean my shoe off under the desk hoping no one would see. However, within minutes everyone was complaining about the smell and looking at each other.

"SSSHHH!!!" the teacher shouted from her desk and looked up.

She looked directly at me then down under my desk at the smeared dog shit and went berserk. She actually mimed the word fuck and then remembered where she was. She marched up grabbing me by the scruff of the neck and then began gagging as the smell hit her.

"Go and get a mop and bucket and get that mess cleaned up!" she bawled at the top of her voice.

I spent the next hour rearranging the shit as the other kids sat nearly being sick. The job done, I sat down, and the teacher came over and started giving me a lecture on my attendance and such. She finished her sermon by telling me to pull my socks up. I took this literally and began pulling my socks up because they were after all around my ankles. She wrongly reacted to this innocent gesture as an insult and threw me out of the class for insubordination. I was baffled as to why I was ejected for doing what she said. The irony is had I have attended school more often I would have understood she was talking metaphorically. I stood outside the classroom feeling dejected and if I am truthful, baffled.

As the smell of the food from the dining hall wafted past me, my stomach rumbled, and I imagined the lovely food the other kids would soon be tucking into. My thoughts were broken by the appearance of the Headmaster, Mr Sefton, who enquired as to why I was standing outside class.

"I don't know, Sir," I answered him honestly, "the teacher told me to pull my socks up, and when I did, she threw me out."

He worked out in an instant what had happened and shot me a pitiful smile. He went into the class and spoke with my teacher and came back out a minute later.

"Come with me, Edward," he said walking towards his office.

"The cane," I thought, "it's got to be."

Now I was scared. I duly followed him at a pace that suggested I would rather not.

"Come on, hurry," he said.

We arrived at his office, and he sat down and pointed to the chair opposite

"Sit down, Edward" he ordered.

I sat down wondering why he didn't just get on with it, but then I thought it might give me the opportunity to bluff my way out.

"Sir, I Sir errr," blurted out, "it was an acc..."

"It's okay, you are not in trouble," he said, trying to calm me.

"I'm not?" I thought, now I was confused.

Just then, there was a knock on his door, and his secretary came in with a cup of coffee. She placed it on his desk and left. It smelt delicious and given we never had coffee at home I felt like reaching over and drinking it.

"Look, Edward, why is it that you miss so much time at school?"

I didn't know how to answer.

"Are your parents ill?" he asked.

"No Sir," I replied, trying to draw my eyes away from the coffee.

He went on to ask numerous questions about my home life and domestic situation and trying to put a finger on why I was so scruffy, and my attendance was so poor. He raised his eyebrows at some of my answers which he obviously had concerns about.

Finally, he said, "Edward, when did you last eat?"

I shrugged my shoulders and said, "Last night, Sir."

"Haven't you eaten breakfast?" he asked, looking alarmed.

"No Sir," I answered truthfully.

"Okay, that is all," he said, "you can return to class now".

As I got up to leave he said, "would you like that coffee?"

"Yes, I would Sir," I answered with excitement.

"Go on then," he said.

I picked it up and gulped it down including the skin on the top. It was all worth it for that. That teacher had concerns, and what he did with them I will never know, but I know he had compassion which in that time of my life was very thin on the ground.

In my endless outings with my mates, we would often flirt with danger not out of bravado but in total ignorance of what the consequences were if things went wrong and sometimes they did go wrong with painful results.

One autumn night a gang of us were standing around a small bonfire in Mick Price's garden. It was only a small fire his dad had left after burning some old rubbish. We all began poking sticks into the fire and generally playing about when someone threw an empty hairspray aerosol container onto the fire we all scattered just in time to hear the boom as the can exploded. This was really fun, so we all went in search of more cans and began throwing them into the fire in ever increasing quantities, and then binding two cans together for real effect. Such was the force when the last two cans were thrown in that it blew the fire out completely, or so we thought. In a moment, someone in the gang produced a can of petrol from their dad's garage.

From this moment, my fate was sealed. We began pouring the petrol into rusty cans and then throwing it into the fire the effect was instantaneous. For some reason by instinct or whatever I still don't know to this day, but as Mick Price was filling his can, I moved over to his younger brother Billy and pulled him back behind me. In that same moment, Mick threw his can of petrol at the fire. Like lightning, the flame from the fire ran up and ignited the can of petrol still in his hand. He reacted as anybody would have and threw the can, unfortunately for me, the contents went all over me, and in a second I was in flames.

I felt a searing pain that was so intense on my right calf that I nearly passed out and then I began to run. This was not a conscious thought it was my body reacting to the pain trying to get away from whatever it was. I have a vague recollection of my friends' horror as they looked on. At this point, I was not aware that the petrol had gone over my back as well because luckily, I had a thick coat on and it had not burned through. Someone with good sense managed to bring me down on the ground and beat the flames out with a piece of old carpet. The nylon trousers I was wearing had melted into the flesh on my calf, the skin was hanging like a sheet from my leg, and there was nauseating smell of burning flesh and petrol. No one thought to pour cold water on to my burnt leg they were not aware of first aid than as they are now, so the nylon kept burning.

Needless to say, I went into shock, and for a while, the pain ceased, and during this time my mates dad had bundled me into his car after alerting my parents. He intended taking me to hospital but as the real pain set in and I began to howl he diverted to the nearby ambulance station. The ambulance crew took one look and loaded me into the back and took off lights flashing and sirens blaring.

The relief of the pain killing drugs on my arrival at the hospital was such that I thought that was it but it wasn't it was only the beginning, and I suffered months of treatment. I shall never forget the pain, and I bear the scar on my right calf today.

"You stupid little sod," my mother said chastising me, although she never shouted because she realised I had learned my lesson.

Though being burnt curtailed my wanderings for a while, I was soon back with my mates, and we were soon up to no good.

I was out playing with a lad who was a bit of a spoilt brat one day when he told me that a family who lived in the road had gone away on holiday. Spoilt Brat hung around with the lad whose family had gone away, so I knew he was telling the truth.

"If you want you can go in his house as long as no-one sees you," Spoilt Brat said to me.

He had my attention immediately.

"Why have you got the key," I enquired.

"No", he replied, "he has left the back-window open for me."

I was away in a moment to get the rest of the gang. When I returned with two of the other lad's, Spoilt Brat looked rather uncomfortable.

"Only us four can go in", he said with a weak determination.

"Okay", we all agreed.

We set off down the track that ran parallel to the railway line at the back of our houses. It was so overgrown that it would have been near impossible for anyone to spot us, and this we had used to our advantage many times in our little forays up and down the railway lines. We hopped over the fence with ease and ran the short distance down the garden to the house. Spoilt Brat pulled on the window and nothing happened it was firmly shut.

"He promised", Spoilt Brat said with a desperate look on his face.

He knew if he had been leading us up the garden path (literally!) that he would get a good thumping. In a moment, he pulled on the other window, and it popped open.

"See, I told you", he said with a smug look on his face.

Okay, we hurried, get in. We all climbed in and stood there staring, wondering what to do now we were here. Then we began exploring. I marvelled at how beautiful the house was and wished my house was like this. We went up to the lad's bedroom, I looked at all his nice things, football boots and scarves. He even had nice carpet on the floor. I even lay on his bed, which he had all to himself. We all moved back the downstairs; the niceties were over it was time for some real action. At this point, Spoilt Brat began to get nervous and started suggesting it was time to leave.

One of our gang got hold of him, "Look you. We break into houses all the time without anybody knowing, not like this one where the window has been left open".

It was a complete lie we had never broken into any house, but it made us sound tough to Spoilt Brat.

"And anyway, we're not leaving here empty handed", he added.

"Wow, look at this", one of our trio whispered across the room.

We all scurried over to see a box full of money in the drawer of a wall cabinet. There were notes and coins of every denomination. I had never seen that much money. We all looked at the cash flabbergasted.

"Imagine how many action men I could get with this lot", I thought, "I could even possibly by myself a new chopper bike".

A whisper came from the kitchen, "Forget that look at this".

One of the gang was standing there with the fridge door open. We all peered inside to be greeted by a huge chocolate bar.

"Shall we," someone urged from the back.

"Bloody right," we all agreed.

"But they will know," Spoilt Brat protested.

"You tell your mate you took it," we urged Spoilt Brat.

"Okay," he relented.

The chocolate bar was quickly shoved inside somebody's jumper, and we made off down the garden to share our ill-gotten gains. Taking the money never entered our heads it simply wasn't an option we even considered for a moment. We thought we had pulled off the robbery of the century.

"I told you we had broken into houses before", I lied to Spoilt Brat.

I look back on this incident with a real sense of guilt but had Spoilt Brat not practically invited us in we would never have gone into the house in the first place.

I also wonder if lads of our age today would be so innocent as to leave cash and take a chocolate bar. I thought at the time I was in the big league of criminals and really smart.

Being the hardened professional housebreakers, we thought we were; we decided to put our newly acquired talents to the test a few weeks later. I had discovered that my sister, Mary, was babysitting for a neighbour one night. So, we decided that we would use this opportunity to play at trick on one of the lads who for want of a better word was a bit slow on the up take.

As usual, we used the well-trodden path that ran parallel to the railway track and the gardens to launch our assault; it was simply a matter of hopping over the fence into the backyard and through the back door. As was pre-planned I was to go in with half-wit in tow. I moved with the stealth of a panther through the darkened shadows of the garden when there was an almighty crash and a yelp of pain from Half–wit.

"Shhh," I said to him keep quiet.

"I walked into a wheelbarrow," he said in a hushed moan.

Half-wit had no idea that my sister was babysitting, it would spoil the plan if he knew. I opened the back door, and we slipped in. I stopped at the living room door and peeped through the keyhole. My sister was sitting watching the television in ignorant bliss. I beckoned Half-wit to follow me up the stairs, which he did with the grace of an elephant.

On reaching the upstairs landing, I told Half-wit to go and look in the bedroom, which he did and I then moved down the stairs like lightning with not a sound. I could hardly stifle my laughter as I reached the back door. I opened it and quietly stepped outside. I then slammed the door with all the force I could muster and ran.

I leapt the fence where all the rest of the gang were waiting. They were nearly peeing their pants with laughter. The effect was instantaneous; all the lights in the house went on it looked like Blackpool Illuminations as my sister came out to investigate the noise. Then Half-wit's face appeared at the bedroom window. He looked desperate and trapped, as he was when we heard the back door being locked. In all this, I gave no thought to my poor sister. But we lay there in the darkness laughing. It must have been nearly twenty minutes before Half-wit emerged from the house and he had revenge on his face. I knew it was futile to protest, so I let him hit me and feigned injury, so he stopped.

"Do you want to come to the shops?" my mother asked me.

"Yes," I said at the prospect of getting some sweets or even better a coloured torch. I should have known better, on reaching the shops she diverted into a small road and thrust me through the door.

"Give him a short back and sides," she instructed the barber and promptly left to go and get her shopping.

"Sit down and be quiet," the barber said looking at me like I was something off his shoe.

He was a stern looking man with British Army advertising posters all over the shop walls. He ritually began inspecting my head for lice as on one occasion he had found some and chased me out of the shop to wait in the doorway for my mother.

"Get your mother to clean your hair," he shouted, "and don't come back here until she has."

He then began telling every customer who came into the shop that I was lice ridden. Fortunately, I passed the test this time and was declared louse free, and he began attacking my mop of hair with his clippers.

"Can I just have a bit off becau..." I tried to say.

"Shut up," he cut in, "you will get what you're given."

The savage assault with clippers over, he slapped a hand full of Brylcreem onto my head. He put in an awkward part and told me to be quiet and wait for my mother.

It was always the same I would be towed off to the barbers once my hair had reached the point where it could no longer be ignored; it often looked like I had swallowed a hand grenade. I recall with horror even to this day, when my parents decided the barbers were too expensive and they purchased a pair of clippers themselves. I was to be the guinea pig. Very predictably they left me half-bald, and I had to be taken to the barbers to have the best of a bad job sorted out.

I had been suffering from a toothache for a few days when my mother told me she was taking me to have it looked at, at the dentist.

"No, I don't want to go," I protested, sensing it might involve even more pain.

"He only wants to look that's all," she said, "and then we can come straight home."

"Only look? Promise?" I replied

"Yes," she said.

We walked up to Moreton Village, or The Cross as it was known, and down a side street to the children's clinic and dentist. At that time, they were Government run and very intimidating for a child. We sat in the waiting room, and I fidgeted nervously when I heard a child screaming!

"What's that?" I asked in fear, "I want to go home."

"That's not the dentist," my mother said, trying to calm me.

"What is it then?" I cried unconvinced by her answer because I was sure it was from the dentist.

"It's the clinic," she replied.

OK, I thought, let's see. Ten minutes later a woman came out with a little girl who looked like she was drunk and being supported.

"What's up with her?" I whispered.

"She's tired," my mother replied.

Oh, I thought it must be okay if she can sleep.

"Edward!" shouted a very stern looking man with silver hair and glasses.

My mother grabbed my hand and led me into the dentist surgery. The surgery had some very strange smells about it and some very weird tools that looked like instruments of torture.

"Get in the chair!" the silver haired Dentist ordered.

As it was too high, my mother lifted me in. I didn't like this man one bit. He spoke to my mother then ordered me to open my mouth. I did as I was told.

"Wider!" he barked at me.

He poked and prodded inside my mouth and then I felt a sharp pain and screamed out.

"Okay, Okay," said the dentist, "I see it."

"See what?" I thought, my mind racing.

The dentist nodded and began sorting through the instruments of torture. This wasn't looking good, and I sensed something bad was going to happen. A woman entered the room and then my mother said she had to go to the toilet! As I was about to protest, a big rubber mask was pressed over my face with the most nauseating smell coming from it. It was the stern looking dentist, and the woman was holding my legs. I fought as hard as I could. I was writhing about trying to get the mask off. These two, bad, people were trying to kill me, while my mother was in the toilet, I thought, but she will be back and stop them. The more I struggled, the tighter the mask was pushed on to my face. I began to feel odd and felt like I was floating and then blackness.

"Edward, Edward!" it was that Dentist who had been trying to kill me.

He has changed his mind, I thought, or my mother had stopped him. I felt sick, and my mouth was hurting.

"It's all done," my mother said.

"What's all done?" I asked confused.

"You've had that rotten tooth taken out," she said smiling.

I had been set up and I never even saw it coming. They had gassed me and removed my rotten tooth.

As was always the way, my mother's debts began to catch up with her, and she took the only escape route open to her, she ran off and left us. Most of the debts came as great shock to my father, though on reflection I think he must have been very naïve or turning a blind eye because my mother could not sustain her drink habit with the money he gave her.

My mother had got into arrears on almost everything including the rent, electricity and gas. The electricity was about to be cut off, and we were all facing possible eviction from the council.

When I asked where my mother had gone, I was told she had gone away for a while.

"Where to?" I enquired.

"Away that's all," came the answer.

I knew why because I had heard my elder sisters discussing it with my father. I recall that our daily habits changed as one of my elder sisters took charge. We were all given a wash and had our teeth brushed which was totally alien to me, and what's more, we were sent to school. I quite liked the order that had descended on to the house and our lives. I thought that if this continued then maybe I would be smartened up even further and given new shoes and pants, possibly long ones. I missed having my mother around, but I welcomed this attention to cleanliness that I had been shown.

My mother returned home less than a week later, and disorder came back to our lives as it had never been away. I assume my father settled the debts and paid more attention to the bills.

For a hard day's work picking potatoes, the local farmer paid seventy pence, or the market garden paid eighty pence for cutting and dying flowers. I would spend more time at either one of these two places rather than go to school. Besides the wages, there was one other perk in the way of stolen potatoes. The ruse was as the farmer went away to take care of other business we would all load our sacks and throw them behind a hedge in the next field only to return in darkness and retrieve them.

However, farmers are not stupid, and one night, as my mates and I returned for our loot, the farmer was waiting for us. As we approached in the darkness, he called out from the shadows screaming that we were all fired and not to return the next day.

"You thieving little bastards!" he shouted.

We all scattered in every direction. But after we got home we realised that the farmer could not possibly have known who was who in the pitch black, so, we showed up for work the next day as though nothing had happened.

"Were you the little bastards who have been robbing my spuds?" he said, as we walked into his yard.

"No," we all protested, "we wouldn't do that."

"Okay," he relented, "but if I catch any of you stealing, I will ring your necks understood."

"Yes," we said in unison.

I know now that if the farmer had actually wanted to catch us, he could have, but his warning worked, for a while anyway.

The local chocolate factory permeated the delicious smell of chocolate and biscuits from every crack, and for hungry urchins, the temptation was too much. Even though I had more to lose than anyone else did with my father working there, I still went along with the gang on raids for chocolate goodies.

Cadbury's was vast, but its position was perfect for us as the railway line and path ran parallel to it, and so we could get in undercover. The only real downside was the local station master who shouted out the window that he was calling the police if he spotted us at all. The security for the entire factory was two ancient men who would take a ride around in their van every once in a while. They never stood a chance because we always posted a look out who would give a low whistled that they were coming and so we would take cover behind all the old pallets and other junk that lay about. As all our raids took place under cover of darkness, the security men never stood much hope in catching us.

I loved the anticipation of the raids, not only was it daring but the rewards were lots of chocolate fingers. On one particular raid, we had agreed that we should venture a bit further into the factory. The only downside to this was that the men who worked in the factory were not elderly like the security staff and so it would be harder to escape should we be spotted.

On this raid, there were three of us, Reg, Mick and I, which was just about the right number. We moved with a well-practised ease down the railway track. It was only about 9, o'clock but cold and wet, so there was hardly anybody about. We reached the chocolate factory through the station and then climbed the fence using the station's waiting room. Without a hitch, we eased ourselves up on to the loading bay platform. We stayed quite still for a few moments to make sure no one had spotted us. It had happened before when a few of the lads had climbed up one of the men from the factory had been having a sly smoke, in the darkness, he shouted out, and they all ran. It was unlikely that he had reported it, as he would have given his own hiding place away.

Moreton Station and Cadbury's Factory

We pulled the large metal door leading to the factory open a few inches and then moved back into the shadows and once again waited. This was the worst part because once we went into the factory, we would be exposed to the noise and bright lights. There was no movement, and nobody had come to see why the door was open. We moved forward and peeped around the door. There were couple men in their white overalls in the distance, so they posed no threat. Like lightning, we moved into the nearest trolley packed with chocolate biscuits, and all grabbed a couple of packets each. I thought my heart was going to stop. In the distance, we looked, as one of the workers pointed us out to his colleague, and they both started running towards us.

We ran back through the door and leapt off the loading bay platform in one easy movement, but I had made a fundamental mistake. I had forgotten to tuck my jumper into my trousers to stash the loot, and I dropped a packet of biscuits. I cursed, as my treats hit the floor there was no time to stop and pick them up. We scaled the fence by way of the station waiting room and dropped down to the sanctuary of the railway track.

The men from the factory appeared at the door, and we began laughing at them.

"You little bastards," they retaliated.

"I know your dad," one of them shouted, as we made a way down the track to scoff our biscuits.

This concerned me did they really know who I was and did they know my dad? I decided that he was just bluffing and if he did, I would deny it anyway. The thought left my head as I tucked into my biscuits.

Like birds leaving the nest one by one, my elder sisters began to move out and set up their own homes. While this gave us all more room, it also meant that we would be left to our own devices. I hated it when my sisters questioned me as to where I had been and what I had been up to. But I also understood and to a degree realised that they would keep me on the straight and narrow and not let me fall into a life of committing serious crimes. With that authority evaporated. I was most certainly on a slippery slope. But lucky for me, fate played its hand.

One of our gang told me that his brother had joined the army cadets.

"Where is it?" I asked. "What do they do?" I enquired.

"You get to shoot guns and go away on camps with them," he replied.

"They also teach you how to do commando raids without being seen," he added.

We all realised how useful this training would be, so we all decided we would give it ago.

The cadets paraded every Monday and Thursday evening at a little hut a few miles from our homes. We all jumped the bus one Thursday to see if we could join. I had no idea at the time the influence this night would have on me now and later on in life.

A now dilapidated cadet hut

I was below the minimum age to join by a year, but my mate's brother had told me to lie as there was no way they could check it out. As we approached the cadet hut, all the cadets were parading outside the hut. They all turned and looked at my mates and I as we approached. I wasn't so sure it was such a good idea at that moment, but I would not be the first one to walk away and suffer the piss-taking that would surely follow.

"And who are you?" bellowed the pot-bellied man who was standing in front of the cadets with a crown on his jumper, which I later learned was the rank of sergeant major.

We all offered our names.

"What do you want?" he asked.

"To join the cadets," we answered.

"How old are you?" he said pointing at me.

"Thirteen, Sir," I replied not knowing if I should call him sir.

"Good lad," he said, "you will always call me sir. Go and wait outside my office he instructed."

We duly trudged in like sheep.

A few moments later the pot-bellied sergeant major reappeared.

"Come into the office," he said, sitting himself behind a faded grubby desk.

The office had old photographs of soldiers in various poses and recruitment posters hanging off the walls. The place reeked of tobacco, and everything was tinged yellow with nicotine, rather like my house I thought.

Pot Bellied lit himself a cigarette and drew deeply on it and then exhaled the smoke at us.

"Listen," he said looking at no one in particular, "I want you to know this is the real army it's not a kid's playground and if you have come here for some fun your wasting your time."

We all looked at each dumb founded that was precisely why we had come, but we all nodded anyway. The door to the office opened, and another soldier walked in, Pot Bellied hauled himself up right and stubbed his cigarette out.

"Evening Sir," he said saluting.

"I was just reading these new recruits the riot act. That's the commanding officer," he said, as the man walked back out of the door.

The Commanding Officer carried the aura of a soldier, he was smart, clean and had that authoritarian look about him. Even though I was somewhat ignorant of army life, I sensed that this man was what it was really about and not the overweight, smoking, Sergeant Major. We were shown around and talked to the other cadets who treated us like something they had wiped off their shoes; this was my first taste of the pecking order I saw when I joined the army as an adult. A lad a few years older than me, with the rank of sergeant, called everybody to parade, and they all filed into an adjoining room and formed up into three ranks. We raw recruits looked on bewildered until the sergeant told us to join the rear rank.

The Commanding Officer walked into the room, and the pot-bellied Sergeant Major brought the assembled cadets to attention. That is except the new boys, we didn't have a clue what he was on about, but we quickly followed suit. He walked around inspecting each cadet picking out faults and giving praise where he thought it was deserved. He came around to the back row and stood in front of me. I felt petrified and vulnerable being under the spotlight. In a move, I only came to understand and appreciate years later the Commanding Officer moved forward as though straightening my arms and whispered into my ear see me after the parade.

I sloped off to his office after the parade and tapped on his door come in. He beckoned from inside. I walked in and made a feeble attempt at coming to attention. He dismissed it with a wave of his hand and said, "Don't worry about that for now."

"The reason I want to speak to you is apart from getting your hair cut, which you are going to do?" he said nodding.

"Yes, sir," I agreed.

"It's your neck, young man, it's filthy, isn't it?"

"Yes, sir," I answered assuming he was right because I couldn't actually remember the last time I had had a bath.

"You must wash every day, not just for cadets, it's very important, do you understand me?"

"Yes, sir," I replied truthfully.

Because it hit me like a bolt of lightning that I was dirty and if I could improve in this, life might get better at school. With one last caring thought the commanding officer then told me to say he was enquiring about my age should the other lads want to know why I had been called into his office.

I owe that man a lot because from that moment on I really became aware of my own hygiene and the real need to keep clean. But on the downside, it also highlighted the desperate filthy condition of my home life, and I began to look at it through different eyes and question why we had to live as we did. I began to realise that it all came down to my mother's drinking and my father's indifference to how we lived and how we were raised as long as he was all right.

Once we had been issued uniforms, which I relished because I was an equal with my mates not scruffy or different in any way we began going away for weekends and two-week summer camps to the Isle of Man and such like. I had never really been anywhere apart from Wales with an underprivileged children's charity, so the Isle of Man was a big adventure.

Along with a few of the other lads in our road, I had started to camp out in the back garden during the summer months, at weekends mostly but almost permanently during the summer holidays. None of our parents had any idea, but sleeping in the tents that were erected in the garden was the last thing on our minds.

Once it had passed midnight, we would emerge from our tents like ghosts in the night ready to explore the twilight world uninterrupted, as long as we weren't caught. This is where the cadets played another important role they taught us well in the art of stealth camouflage and concealment. We learned how to move in darkness without being seen how to remain still so a person standing a few feet away would remain unaware of your presence. They also showed us the importance of wearing clothing that could not be seen or heard like coats that made a noise when walking. We all listened eagerly soaking in the lessons like sponges. The instructors marvelled at our enthusiasm. Little did they know that the things they were teaching us were being put in to practice that same night. To put the icing on the cake the cadets even supplied us with commando type woollen hats and face paint to camouflage ourselves.

After emerging from the tent just past midnight on one hot summer night, three of us padded down the road to await another lad whose mother had refused to let him out. We had on most of our uniforms from cadets complete with camouflage paint on our faces. We were virtually invisible in the darkness to an unwary eye. We settled down on a small grass field opposite the lad's house and waited for him to show his face at the window, and as pre-arranged we would then show ourselves. I moved up to the window and listened to hear if his parents were still up.

I could hear shuffling and then the sound of a television being turned off. Then in an instant, I heard the front door being opened. I dropped to the ground and stayed perfectly still only a few feet from the step; I was almost certain that I was going to be caught as the lad's father put the milk bottles on the step. He was so close I could smell him, I did not even take a breath, and I was waiting for his hand to yank me up, but nothing happened he closed the door and went back inside. When it was safe, I re-joined the others. They could hardly contain their laughter. Did you see how close he was I said not believing how lucky I had been. We all come to realise that the instructors had been right; if the eye wasn't looking for something, in particular, it would concentrate on the job in hand. It was rather like watching a film at the cinema while the characters are talking, not many people look at the background. This real lesson in the art of concealment had been like opening Pandora's Box for us.

Our fascination with the, very dangerous, electrified railway nearly led to one of us being killed on a number of occasions only this night our newly acquired talent in the art of concealment also played a part in it.

The train service would usually finish around midnight, and we would see the last train pass us just afterwards. I have analysed the events of this night many times in my life, and I can say with my hand on my heart it still makes my blood run cold. Two of my mates and I had just emerged from the tent after midnight and had decided to wait by the track for the last train to pass so we could follow up the track unhindered. The last train came by, and we started moving, walking on the railway sleepers because they made less noise than the stone.

"What's that up ahead?" Mick whispered into my ear.

We crouched down and watched, there was movement ahead of us, near to the station.

"It's workmen," I whispered back to Mick. I indicated with my hand to fall back, and so we walked back to wait for the men to finish whatever they were doing on the station. After retreating to a safe distance, we sat down nonchalantly in the middle of the railway track and started talking in whispers. Mick who was with me was halfway through a story when all hell let loose. I was almost blown from the track by a blurring horn. I turned around to see the ominous, yellow, face of a train. In a split second, I along with the other two had launched myself off the track on to the nearby embankment. None of us had even heard the train coming towards us. We had all come close to losing our lives in a split second, but we did not learn our lesson.

We continued to flirt with danger as far as the railway line was concerned. I look back now and wonder what held our fascination but also left us totally ignorant to the fact that we were dicing with death. One warm summer's night, my mate Mick and another one of the gang were sitting on the fence at the back of Mick's garden casually throwing springs from the many old mattresses that had been dumped on to the live rail. It was fun watching them blow into the air with a bang and puff of smoke, hence the nickname genie, we had given to our favourite past time. It was dark, so the effect of the wire spring hitting the live rail only highlighted the flash. Inevitably we all tried to outdo each other as to who could make the biggest bang, so we then began throwing two wires springs entwined.

"Watch this then," said Mick, holding a strand of about four wire springs. The wires hit the line with a flash and loud bang. "Quick get down," Mick shouted, as the lights began to go on in the houses nearby as the occupants came out to see what was going on. We lay still until it all went quiet again and then re-emerged.

"Right no more," I said to Mick, "otherwise we will get caught."

I was worried because the kitchen light had gone on in my own house.

"One last go," Mick replied, "because I'm going in any way."

"Okay," I said back, "but let's make it a good one then we will scarper." I began pulling wires from the mattress determined to show the other two what a real genie looked like when I caught sight of Mick staggering towards the railway line with a huge length of chicken wire fencing rolled up into a ball. It was so big that I could only see his legs. With one last final heave, he threw it onto the live rail. The following explosion threw us all back such was the force, but worse was the blinding flash that left us unable to see. Like a hare caught in car head lights we sat stunned unable to do anything, and then instinct took over, and we began to run blindly as none of us could see a thing.

Somehow, we all managed to make it out of the garden and hide in the shed. People were coming out of their houses to investigate.

"You stupid get, Mick," I whispered. "What did you do that for," trying to distance myself from any trouble heading our way. We could hear our names being called by our parents, but we stayed low. After about 20 minutes when all had gone quiet, and we could see again we decided to make a move.

"Not a word to anyone," I said to Mick and the other lad with us.

"If anyone asks we were at the park," Mick replied.

I slipped back into my house through the back door trying not to make any noise only to be confronted by one of my sisters.

"Where have you been?" she said loud enough for my mum and dad to hear.

"Round the park," I offered with an innocent look.

"Well who has been throwing things on the railway line?" she enquired further.

"I don't know," I answered, "I haven't been near the lines."

"Well someone has because there was a huge bang before and it lit up all the house roofs for miles."

"Oh, I saw that when I was in the park, with Mick," I replied trying to strengthen Mick's alibi.

Thinking she was giving me some gossip my sister dropped her line of enquiry and told me in great detail about the huge explosion and how the entire street was out. She even began naming suspects who I knew were entirely innocent. I agreed with her, happily knowing that I was now in the clear.

I think if it hadn't been for our tear away lifestyle things would have been totally miserable because when I was running the streets up to no good, I forgot the situation at home and at school. I think young minds have the ability to just live in the here and now, rather like when a baby hurts itself and then forgets pretty quickly. When I was with my mates, I was happy, and that was down to the freedom to roam about. We all got into the odd squabble and fight and played tricks on each other but they were soon forgotten unless they were particularly nasty. Being blessed with two clay quarries where we lived, we would sometimes ride to Carr Lane quarry which was a bit further on our bikes we had knocked up from old parts from the rubbish tip.

We pulled up to the edge one hot summer's day looking down into the abyss of the quarry and the very steep bank that led to the bottom. Mick's brother, John, was just in front of me stood on the ground straddling his bike when I nudged him forward with the tyre of my bike. I really didn't expect anything other than to scare him but he just shot off the edge with his balls banging on the cross bar of the bike, all the way down to the bottom. By this time, I knew the consequences of what I had done and was making good my escape. I could hear him as the bike bounced from boulder to boulder and his balls acting as the suspension. He sounded like a female opera singer as the bike would hit another boulder and then level out only to hit another one. I was some distance away but could still hear the high pitched shrill. Finally, silence descended because I was so far away or he had reached his destination. I peddled as fast as I could without sitting on the bike seat once. I arrived home sweating and run straight upstairs where one of my sisters collared me.

"What have you been up to?" she asked, seeing my face, as red as a farmer's arse.

"Nothing," I lied, "I've been on a message."

Sensing that I rarely told the truth she left it at that. I went into the bedroom thinking up excuses as to why I had practically given John a sex change. I was waiting for the inevitable knock on the door, but nothing came. I was puzzled? So, I ventured out the front door to see if they were back. Judging by the bikes on Mick's front they were! I thought John might be in the hospital all cooling his balls in a cold bath but I wasn't sure, so I decided to bite the bullet and go and see. As I turned in to the alleyway at Mick's house, John was walking out a bit like John Wayne in fact. I turned to run, but despite him having balls like space hoppers he was on me and grabbed me by the scruff of the neck.

"You little bastard!" he yelled.

"It was an accident," I pleaded, waiting for his fists to start pummelling me, but instead he grabbed me by the ankles all six stone of me and began swinging me around. With my skinny frame and wild hair, I must have looked like a toilet brush. As the blood rushed to my head and the G-force built up, he gained more and more speed. I think even the well-established head lice were departing my hair.

"Little bastard!" I could just hear as the same scenery passed me time and time again.

I could hear someone saying, "Look at the dust coming off him," as I passed by.

Then I was flying through the air watching the ground underneath me. The landing was a blare as I knocked the wind out of myself and swallowed half the lawn. John was standing over me.

"Serves you right," he said.

"Fuck off!" I shouted back, "It couldn't have hurt that much?"

But it did. Apparently, John's balls looked like the colours of a rainbow. I think he has kids now, but I am not sure. It was strange because despite what he had done to me in revenge John was the voice of reason, he was the thinker, and he would discourage us from doing things that looking back would clearly have injured us or someone else.

You would pick a brick up to toss through someone's green house, and John would grab the brick from you and say, "Don't do that! How would you like it."?

He would then lecture you on why it was a bad idea and sometimes he did make us see the error of our feral ways.

We were stood by the railway line down the quarry one day when we decided to start throwing mud balls at the passing trains. We would get a handful of wet clay and squeeze it into a hard ball and as the train passed throw it at the windows watching the passengers jump thinking it was a stone. Coupled with the trains speed and our throwing ability it would hit very hard, and I suppose there was a chance it could have smashed the window, but such physics were beyond our thoughts. As the train approached, we all threw our mud balls screaming in delight as they hit the target and the train blared out its horn in protest at the attack.

"Ha ha!" we yelled, laughing as I turned to wash the mud off my hands, there stood six feet away, was a policeman and behind him his car that he had drove up, and during the din and excitement we hadn't seen him.

He grabbed us and demanded our names and addresses. By this time, we were all shaking with fear. Start heading home he shouted, and I will be there with your parents. He drove off down the path, and we began the walk back to the gallows. Each step brought us closer to something nasty. As we turned in to our road parked outside my house was the police car, so I was first to be hung! I decided to go around the back and try and make a low-profile entrance. My sisters were in the garden and couldn't detain their delight at my predicament.

"Oohhh, you've had it," they said with utter joy on their faces.

I peeked through the kitchen window and saw the policeman talking to my mum, they both looked angry. My fate was sealed, so I thought I might as well get it over with.

I opened the door, and my mum said, "What have you been doing?"

Well, she knew because the policeman had just told her, so I decided silence was my best option so as not to refresh her mind again. She grabbed me and began smacking me much to the policeman's delight because he had a big grin on his face. It wasn't hurting too much, but I thought it best to add some screams of pain so they could see justice done. The beating was short lived however because within seconds clouds of thick dust began filling the kitchen off my clothes to such an extent that the policeman and my mum began coughing as she started losing sight of her target. That was enough to draw the punishment to an end, and I was ordered upstairs and told I was not going to get any dinner. I wasn't getting any before I threw the mud, I thought.

After being made to stay in for a few days, my tether was cut, and I was out and about once more. As was normal in the summer months we would spend every weekend camping out in one of the gardens, though camping was really the last thing on our minds. After a short nap, we climbed out from our tent just after midnight when most people had gone to bed. There were only three of us so we decided we would raid Cadbury's first to fill our bellies and then go down to the local beach where the courting couples parked up for a bit of fun. We were dressed in our cadet's uniforms complete with camouflage face paint and commando style woollen hats. We hopped over the fence on to the railway line as quietly as a church mouse and made our way to Cadbury's once more. We climbed on to the station's railway waiting room and dropped down into the Cadbury's factory and made our way over to the door. Carefully I pulled the door slowly open only to be confronted by a group of workers standing on the other side. I don't know who was more surprised them or me, but I didn't hang about to find out I ran and the other two lads quickly followed. Once again, we heard threats and abuse in our trail, but we disappeared and made good our escape. Once on the other side of the station and safely away we all fell about laughing.

So, it was on to the next adventure, the courting couples! With the stealth of world war two commandos, we made our way along the main road towards the beach taking cover every time we saw car headlights in the distance or heard a noise. Even the police cars drove past oblivious of our presence. On arriving at the darkened and deserted beach, we hid in the grass and took cover and waited. There were no cars but given this was the weekend and the night clubs would soon be closing, we knew some cars would soon be arriving with passionate couples aboard.

We didn't have to wait long when the first car approached and parked up in the darkest spot it could find. Cream coloured suits and big red collars were all the rage at that time, and the Bee Gees look was in. The car that had pulled in was a Capri, and we could hear the romantic music coming from within, this guy certainly knew how to treat a lady. We grabbed a handful of turf and soil and began crawling towards the car on reaching the exhaust pipe we started stuffing the mud in to block it off, this done we crawled back to our hide and waited.

After ten minutes or so the sounds of moaning began coming from the car over the music. Time for phase two of the operation. As one we ran to the car from the grass screaming and shouting and then climbed on the roof banging with our hands making as much noise as possible. The screams of both the man and woman inside even drowned out our own screaming. The man threw himself over the seat with his pants around his ankles and his stiffened wand still ready for action. The woman was still screaming as she pulled up her underwear. In an instant, the car started with a thump, and all the soil and turf shot out the back. It pulled away, the revs screaming and the car sliding and skidding on the grass. As it hit the tarmac road, it roared off still with no lights on and the woman screaming.

We ran off towards the path that would lead us to the railway line laughing that we had just ruined a night of passion and nearly frightened a poor couple half to death. The seriousness of what we had done and the possible impact never entered our heads. I mean they were probably a young couple and had just enjoyed a night out, and we come along and ruin it. I have sometimes wondered why we occupied our time with such activities and I think it was because we were seeking our own independence and mischief and there was that element of danger about it I suppose. I don't deny we felt good and would laugh at what we got up to but had we really thought about it, we might not have been so cruel.

As money became rare and the poverty began to deepen, our life style inevitably began to change and not just in the obvious ways of our scruffy appearance, but bordering on the farcical. When things like the soap ran out, on the few occasions I had a bath we would use soap powder and then wonder why we had desperately dry skin and angry red rashes on our bodies. When the margarine ran out we would think nothing of using lard on our toast, it made the dry toast moist enough to eat, so that was that. There never seemed to be any milk or if there was there was just enough for my dad's tea in the morning. Sometimes my sisters or I would drink it and then blame each other. My mum would go berserk, and one of us would be sent out to a neighbour to borrow a drop. There was never enough of anything, never enough tea, never enough milk, never enough bread. There should have been ample of everything, I know they were hard times and most people all over struggled but most had at least the bare essentials. We never had toilet paper, and it never occurred to me that we should have done. I thought it was the same all over, people used the Liverpool Echo newspaper to wipe their arses, didn't they?

I never had a toothbrush, and I never cleaned my teeth ever. I thought the primary function of the bath was to put stickleback fish in that I had caught in the local ponds. Cadburys had a series of ornamental ponds designed by Sir Geoffrey Jellicoe, and it was full of stickleback fish so I would fill a milk bottle with them and take them home.

The beautiful ponds at Cadbury's

The once beautiful ponds, now derelict

In my haste to get up to the bathroom one day with my bottle of fish, I slipped on the quarry tiles in the kitchen. The bottle smashed spilling the fish all over the kitchen floor and the glass cut my hand deeply. I lay crying out of fear and in pain. My mum and dad came running out of the living room to see me lying in blood with water everywhere and loads of little fish flipping about.

My dad shouted, "What are you doing now you bloody idiot?" "There's something wrong with you," he added and turned around and went back to watch his horse racing on the telly.

My hand was bandaged with a piece of old cloth and the fish thrown down the toilet. I often wonder how our house even functioned things were so desperate that they even took light bulbs from one room to another because there was only one or two in the whole place. It wasn't just the lack of all these material things it was the lack of emotion and homeliness, it wasn't there, and I knew even at that young age that is was lacking.

Despite the life and good laughs on the street I never felt really happy. It was not possible to be honest because my mother's constant battle to find money for alcohol was also our struggle whether we liked it or not. I don't think she understood that we were part of her addiction we had to undergo the pain and trauma of alcohol dependency through her, if her mood was angry, low and desperate then so was ours by association. If she managed to get money for alcohol then she was happy and so were we on the surface.

Each and every empty space in the house concealed empty bottles tossed aside and hidden. The bottle drained of its contents. I wondered where this money could have been better spent, the things it could have bought. I began to despise even the smell of this obnoxious liquid that was taking so much from us, it had a grip on all our lives and saturated misery into every facet of our being. It corrupted everything without mercy and made our lives a misery and held all of us in its grip through my mother. If it were something I could have physically killed, I would have.

I remember finding a half a bottle of whiskey in the larder as my mother slept in the chair. I looked at it though the glass bottle trying to figure out in my juvenile mind what was contained within it that had such an ability to hold people? I unscrewed the top and began pouring it slowly down the sink with a glowing feeling of revenge, and it felt so good.

"You," I said to this liquid, "have come to nothing."

It would be down the drain doing no damage to anyone, and with a start, I realised my folly and the implications of what I was doing so I stopped screwed the lid back on and returned it to the larder with an inch or so less in the bottle. I felt as though it was now mocking me, it had won again because I couldn't even throw it away. So, there it was if I ever needed proof the alcohol had power over us all.

Why wasn't my father noticing what was going on? Well, the sad fact is he was, he was an educated and intelligent man he was acutely aware of my mother's addiction and for whatever reason chose to ignore or just carry on. Somehow his dinner was always on the table even when ours wasn't, he ate it then went back out to the pub, he got up, went to work and lived his life.

It pains me and makes me feel uncomfortable that he knew our, his children's, predicament and ignored it but that really is the only explanation I have. He was aware that we looked scruffy and our clothes were ragged, and we never got bathed he knew the house was a dirty mess that lacked even the basics for good health and cleanliness. How could he not, he lived there?

He hardly had any real interaction with us, in fact, he had none but the odd shout if we somehow made too much noise or annoyed him with our presence. So, it might have been easy for him to ignore my mother's drinking and all the turmoil that goes with it. I sometimes wonder how different our lives and my mother's life might have been if he had taken a stand, made her seek help and took charge of the finance. But he contributed nothing either physically or emotionally. He never once decorated the house or cleaned up; he left EVERYTHING to my mother and that maybe the reason with ten children, through the years, to cope with, that she sought solace in the only thing available, alcohol.

Across the road from us, a new family had moved in, and they had a son who was around our age but a little strange. He seemed a bit of a loner and didn't really interact with us despite us trying. There was something odd about him though. I watched the first time he was sent to the shops. He literally began spinning all the way down the road with his head tilted back looking at the sky. How he never fell over or hit any cars was a miracle. I stood there, mouth wide open, as he spun out of sight. A few minutes later he reappeared with a bottle of milk in his hand and spun all the way down the road home and through the front door!

A few days later, we were down the quarry when we spotted him in the distance pants down answering the call of nature when we began running towards him intent on finding out more about him and more importantly what made him tick. As we ran he spotted us pulled his pants up and was gone into the nearby trees, we searched, but there was no sign of him. For the first time in a while, we were completely baffled this new boy was an enigma.

A few days later, three of us had descended on the local chippy which had just been taken over by Chinese people who fascinated us because at that time there were none in our little town.

"Hawow," we would greet them, "you Chinky."

Then we would run not for one second considering how offensive our racist remarks were to them.

"Chips with sore finger," instead of salt and vinegar, we shouted laughing think we were really funny.

The Chinese lady behind the counter yelled at us to go away, but we were having fun, so there was no chance. She came from behind the counter a few times, and we ran only to return minutes later. This time we crawled in on our hands and knees so she wouldn't see us behind the counter we sat trying to stifle our giggles. I was looking towards the door when I felt a hand grab me, the Chinese lady had me by the scruff of the neck.

"You want to play?" she said, "You want to play?"

Wallop! One smack around the ear.

"You want me to put you in the fryer?" she said.

"No," I cried, "sorry, sorry."

"You be bad, that where you go," she said.

"Sorry, sorry," I repeated.

It was a done deal as far as I was concerned.

"Out!" she ordered.

I ran wiping my tears away so no one could see I had cried like a baby.

"What happened?" the others asked.

When I told them, they just laughed, but I never told them I had cried.

As we made our way home past the local pub, The Morton Arms, who was spinning up the road, the strange boy from over the road. We took cover behind some trees until he got closer; we weren't going to miss this opportunity to have a closer look at him. As he passed, we lunged and grabbed him.

"What are you doing?" we asked.

"Going to the chippy," he said, "let me go."

"Why do you spin everywhere you little freak?" we enquired.

"Aren't you dizzy?" someone else said.

"No," he replied, "I like it."

It was now dark, so we decided to carry on interrogating him. He didn't show any fear which we found odd, and he even laughed at us.

"I'm going to the chippy," he said, "let me go."

"Not yet," we answered.

Then he blurted out, "I've got something you would like."

Now, this was getting interesting.

"What?" we demanded.

"Come and see," he said, "it's in my shed."

"What is it? A motorbike?" I asked.

"No," he said, "I am not telling. Come and see."

"Okay," we relented, "it better be good and it better not be a trap, or you're dead."

"Let me get the chips, and I will show you."

We escorted Strange Boy to the chippy and then back down the road to his house.

"Wait there, and I will come back out," he said taking the chips in.

"You won't see him again," some laughed.

We waited a few minutes, and to our amazement, Strange Boy reappeared. He scaled the wall to his own garden and unlocked the back gate leading to his brick shed.

"Where is this surprise"? I asked now growing suspicious.

"Have a look through the window," Strange Boy replied.

We walked around in the pitch black to the window, and I put my face up close peering into the darkened shed. I couldn't see anything, then without warning a huge eye came up to the window and blinked.

"Aaahh!" I screamed in fear throwing myself back from the glass nearly fainting.

Strange Boy was beside himself laughing at our scare.

"What's that in there?" we demanded.

"It's a horse," he said casually in reply.

"Whose is it? Where did you get it?" we began bombarding him with questions.

"I bought it from some lad," Strange Boy replied. "He's mine now," he affirmed.

"Get him out so we can have a go," we asked feeling really excited.

I had never had the opportunity of a donkey ride on the beach due to lack of money, and now I wasn't looking a gift horse in the mouth, literally. Strange Boy protested at first, offering to get Ned out the following day.

"No, now," we demanded with authority and a little menace.

Strange Boy began pushing the horse out the shed backwards while we kept our distance. It neighed a few times in protest, but he eventually got it out into the street.

"How much did you buy him for?" I asked Strange Boy.

"Not much," he replied, trying to put off my line of questioning.

I thought if I could somehow manage to buy the horse of Strange Boy, I could knock on my door say to my mum and dad, "Look what I've bought."

They would just hug me and say, "Yeah sure put him in the garden."

As the horse was way taller than us, we took him over to the nearest wall and climbed on to him two at a time. No saddle we were real cowboys! Strange Boy led us through the darkened streets where we thought it was perfectly ok to be riding a horse two up no saddle in the pitch black on a residential street.

"Where did you get that bloody horse?" one man inquired as we trotted past.

"It's mine," Strange Boy told him.

"Like shite, it is," the man shouted back, "get it back, or I am phoning the police. THE POLICE!"

We dismounted like an Apache taking a bullet off a cowboy. Just then some older lads appeared and began aggressively questioning Strange Boy.

"That's not your horse you've robbed it!" they shouted.

"No, I haven't!" Strange Boy yelled back.

"Yeah, you fucking are, you little shit!" they shouted louder.

The horse got spooked and began running towards the chippy where it stopped agitated. A woman appeared who worked at the local stables.

"THAT HORSE IS STOLEN!" she yelled.

We all pointed at Strange Boy and said, "He told us it was his and we were trying to find out where it came from."

We missed out the part where we had been riding it. It was time to say goodbye to Ned and fast, so we made off leaving Strange Boy to his fate. Apparently, the police and owner turned up, and Strange Boy said he had found it wandering about but the horse was returned to its owner.

My home town of Moreton in the 1970's was, I think, typical of any small town up and down the country. It was isolated from the world in the sense that there was no internet, there were no live news reports from around the world as there is now. If something happened in Saudi Arabia, then it was unlikely to reach our lives unless it was a major story. I had never heard of most of the countries that are now mentioned and in our lives like now.

If some big news story happened, it would come up across the TV screen as "NEWSFLASH!" No reporters there within a few hours reporting from the scene. I had never heard of Islam, Judaism or Buddhists. Religion was Sunday School where you got sweets. When I heard my mum say, 'Coloured people', I had an image of them being blue and orange and yellow. No immigration touched our lives.

There were no kebabs or curry restaurants. The most exotic curry was a Vesta curry you had to make up from the powered kit in a box. There wasn't even pizza or Mexican food. This fayre may have been available in places like Metropolitan London but Wirral, no. It was if you were lucky and lived in an ordinary house, egg n' chips, spam, a stew commonly known as "Scouse" and desserts such as Angel Delight.

The mums would go and get the food on a daily basis as not many people even had fridges and the coolest place in the kitchen was a stone slab in the pantry. The mums would go to the butchers and the veg shop and such and buy what they needed for that day. There were no freezers full of food of every description as there is now. The pubs opened at 11am and closed at 3pm until 5pm when they would open again until 10.30pm and even those hours were reduced on Sundays.

Around the holidays such as Christmas and Easter, everything closed for days on end. We had a milk machine in the village where if you were desperate you could pay the extra but at least get some milk. The little kiosk in the village called Les Turner's would sell what we called "loosies" which were cigarettes you could buy individually. The young smokers who wouldn't normally get served in the local tobacconist would exploit this source to get their fags. You even got a match! There's service for you. There were three channels on TV, and even these were only on at certain times of the day if you had a TV at all. There was some kind of innocence to it all or maybe ignorance of living in a smaller world and only dealing with what was happening in your own life.

We were always preoccupied with ways to make money from running errands to the local shops for neighbours to working on the local market gardens, to the farm and even caddying for the golfers on the local golf links. I was at a definite disadvantage due to being rather small in height and about six stone.

One day someone told us about a unit on the local industrial estate that now stood where the old prefab housing had been, and they were taking paper for recycling. We investigated, and sure enough, they would pay a £1 a ton which was a small fortune to us then. So, we built a trolley and began knocking on doors for old newspapers and weighing them in. It was hard work, but we were getting money, and it was going well until word spread, and then more and more kids were collecting, so it got harder and harder with much longer hours and work. We soon realised the game was up due to saturation and as a parting shot, on our last load, we hid a few bricks in the bottom of the paper, collected the money and scarpered, back to the drawing board.

As one door closes, another one opens so they say and this time Mick Price and I hit on the idea of washing the wheels on the cars as they went into the car wash at the local garage. We got permission from the woman in the garage shop, and she let us fill our bucket with hot water, and we started. We made a fortune! The money was pouring in, and we couldn't believe our luck. Being naïve we told the other lads who wanted in on it, but we refused, it was our little business. Two or three weeks later one hot Sunday afternoon we were sat having a break between cars when two older lads came wandering over. One of them picked the bucket up and told us to fuck off it was now their business. We tried to protest but they threatened us, and they meant it, so we wandered off business gone and just to add insult to injury they kept our bucket and sponge. In revenge, we rang the manager of the garage and pretended to be a customer whose car had been scratched, so the two lads got told where to go.

I lived for the freedom of going out roaming about during the night getting up to no good. I think back now, and it was because we owned the place in the sense that there were no adults to tell us what to do, interfere or any worries apart from getting caught which actually added to the excitement of it all. I loved the darkness and the anonymity, being invisible and answering to no one. Even now as an adult I dream about being marooned on an island and surviving all alone. I know I would pine for my wife and children, but it's that isolation and no contact with other people that I find attractive. Don't misunderstand me, I don't hate people but I feel disappointed in the human race, in so much as I see what we are capable of and I realise we are the brightest but also the most primitive species on the planet. I sensed that same feeling later on in my life when I went to war in the Falklands. We used technology that had been invented and created by the best minds to kill each other, oh the irony.

For some reason, the only two people who had managed to camp out one night was Stewart Martindale and me. Stewart had actually been kicked out of the house by his mum who had grown tired of his misbehaviour. As a single mum, she had her work cut out, and it was an attempt to make him realise that sleeping in a warm bed was better than sleeping on a cold step. We had set the tent up in another lad's garden despite the fact he wasn't even camping out with us. There was an old flea infested sofa at the end of the garden and for one reason or another Stewy and I ended up sitting on it. We discussed the world and our futures, which as thirteen-fourteen-year-olds was very unusual for us. We hardly stopped running about to breathe let alone get into a deep conversation.

We sat looking up at the inky black night as people slept and watched as aeroplanes flew over.

Stewart Martindale and the author, still friends

"I wonder if we will ever go on one of those?" Stewy said.

"Fucking right we will," I answered, "I want to see all the world. I want to see Australia and America. In fact, I want to live in America, they have millions of TV channels and massive cars."

Stewy said, "I wonder what it's like when you get to a faraway place?"

He went on to question how it would feel to be in Arab deserts and palm trees. I was enthralled, Stewy was bright, and I liked chatting with him. I had no ambitions career-wise, so, I didn't know how I was going see these places, but somehow, I knew I would.

Halfway through our around the world debate, Stewy said, "I am fucking starving. I haven't eaten for ages can you get me some grub from your house?"

Now he was asking for miracles, but I said I would go and look. So, I sneaked into my house, through the open back door, and found some very old cheese and stale bread and gave it to him. He devoured it down like a boy who hadn't eaten for a long time which is exactly what he was. Stew's hunger pangs numbed for the time being we went on to wondering where our lives would lead us and where we would be if still alive thirty years on?

Well, Stew is married to Karen, with some lovely children. He has his own business and like me has travelled the world, after a stint in the Army!

As the birds began to sing the dawn chorus we retreated to the tent and sleep.

A few nights later, I had been told I couldn't camp out on this particular night for some reason or another, but I arranged with Stewy to come and wake me, as I would sleep on the sofa in the living room and leave the window open. That night I opened the window slightly and lay down on the sofa.

My mum appeared at the door and said, "What are you doing?"

"Sleeping on here," I replied.

"No, you're not," she said, "bed now."

I went upstairs and sat by the bedroom window waiting for Stewy to warn him the game was up. My eyes were heavy, and he hadn't appeared, so, I lay down for a minute. I was woken by the sound of screaming. I couldn't work out what was going on. My mother came running up the stairs.

"You little bastard!" she screamed.

"What?" I protested in all innocence.

"You bloody know what!" she yelled back, "That Stewart Martindale has just reached in through the window and shaken me awake whispering Eddy, Eddy! And when I screamed, he ran off."

My mind was now racing, what could I say?

"Mum, he is mad," I protested. "He's done it someone else's mum the other night," I lied, happy to throw Stewy under a bus to save my own neck.

Just then my dad appeared from the bedroom. "What's going on," he said rubbing his eyes, "I've got bloody work in the morning."

Oh great, I thought, I'm really in the shit now. My mum told him about Stewy, and he went mad.

"If I find out you have been sneaking out with him, you've had it!" he shouted.

"I haven't done anything," I protested, crying, "it's him."

Then my sisters appeared pretending they didn't know what was going on but hoping to drop me further in the shit. All we needed was some lights and popcorn, and we had a complete show, and I was the main act. Eventually, all settled down after I was told I couldn't go out again until I was about thirty or so. Just before I retreated under the coat, which was acting as a duvet, I peeped out the window, and there he was, the bastard Stewy, still running about in the darkness.

Alcohol was to some extent still passing us by as a group of friends. I was used to seeing it in the house but hated it for what it was doing. I began seeing signs of real illness in my mother, she was very thin and becoming prone to coughs and chest infections. She hardly bothered with food anyway, so that combined with her alcohol intake made it a downhill slope.

The lad next door, Trevor, invited me in one night while his elderly Nan, who was living with them, mopped and cleaned the kitchen. I don't why but we never really got invited into their house much, it may have been that I looked like tramp with to them but I had made an attempt at smartening myself up after the CO at army cadets had spoken to me.

Trevor invited me into the back room off the kitchen, and we played about and started watching a program called 'Budgie' about a petty criminal played by Adam Faith. In the program, Budgie was drinking whiskey or some other tipple and had loads of money. We looked on in awe as this cool character took on the law and won. That's us, we thought, we're cool and big drinkers, only we weren't big drinkers because we never touched it.

Our luck was in though, in the back-room Trevor's dad had a cabinet and on the cabinet, were various bottles of booze including whiskey. We got two shots glasses and began pouring whiskey into them and drinking them and flicking our hair as Budgie was. I couldn't believe how cool we were. I had always hated alcohol because of what it had done, but now I realised, with a jolt, I was so wrong, it was incredible, it made you really look good, attractive to girls and more handsome and taller.

Trevor's Nan mopped away in oblivion, and we slugged our fire water and called each other Budgie. We planned to start robbing banks and jewellery stores because it was easy, Budgie did it, and we were as good as him, weren't we? I looked over to Trevor, and his eyes were not right. They were looking in a different direction and glazed over. He was also very blurred and spinning. I went to speak, but only a gurgling noise came out. I began to lose my balance and feel nauseous.

Then, as Trevor bounced off the cabinet and started mumbling something like help, Nan, I headed for the door but missed and fell. I somehow picked myself up, made it into the garden, threw myself over the fence and staggered into the house. By now, I was crying, and my Budgie character had flown leaving a very drunk and pathetic scared child. I burst into the living room where one of my sisters was sat, my mum and dad were out. Even now I remember the look of horror on my sister's face as she looked at me thinking I had been beaten or in an accident. She soon realised what I had been up to but for me the night was over, I passed out.

I woke the next morning to pain in my head and the consequences of the night before. Apparently, my mum and dad had given me salt-water to try and make me sick, but I had simply drunk it and gone back to sleep. The lectures started, and I had to go and face Trevor's dad. We were both made to stay in for weeks, and every time I saw whiskey I felt sick, and I have never been able to drink it to this day.

Life at home continued to be dominated by money or at least the lack of it. We would sometimes go to school, but more often than not we would be hanging around the house or streets, not learning and not getting an education.

It would start early, my mum wondering who she could borrow money off. It was always better to go out and try your own luck at getting money. At least if I was able to get some money, I could spend it on myself. So, I was always eager to get out of the house and go see what the day would bring. Sometimes, though there was treasure to be had closer to home. On this occasion, right under my own nose!

I was looking through a very packed cupboard in the kitchen, searching every nook and cranny when my hand chanced upon something that felt like books. I pulled them out only to see that it was a wad of Green shield stamp books that had been hidden. Green shield stamps were given out at almost all the shops. You could get money off your goods in exchange for them once the book was full which took over 1200 stamps or you could get goods with them such as kettles or a food mixer, but you could also sell them in the shops for cash!

Who these books belonged to, I didn't know, but I suspected it was one of my sisters who was particularly tight with her money, she is still that way today. They couldn't have been my mum's because she would have cashed them long ago. My dilemma now was how many I could steal without it being noticed? I took a few, and then greed got the better of me, so, I took roughly half. Then a few more up my jumper and headed off out the back door with my booty.

I got to the nearest shop that I knew bought them for cash and went in.

"Yes," said the man behind the counter.

"I want to cash these," I said putting the books on the counter.

"Are these yours?" he enquired.

"No, they're me mum's," I lied.

"Who is your mum?" he asked.

"Mrs Lloyd," I replied, not sounding too convincing.

"No, it's not, you thieving little bastard. Get out!" he shouted.

I grabbed the books and ran out. I tried my luck at another shop, and they took the books without question. My pockets stuffed with money, I headed to the chippy, had sausage and chips, with gravy, as I was feeling rather flush. Then for dessert, a bar of happy size and I still had money over, result.

I had completely forgotten about the books, when a few weeks later, as I came into the house, my sister grabbed me by the neck.

"Listen to me, YOU! Have you taken any books out of that cupboard?" she said, pointing at the cupboard where I had taken them from.

"What books?" I protested, "what are you on about?"

She looked at me and said, "I will find out who has taken them, and if it was you, WATCH OUT!"

"I haven't done anything," I said, pretending to be upset at such scandalous accusations.

She let me go. Phew, I had got away with it.

I didn't look on this type of behaviour as dishonest or criminal, to me it was all about survival, looking after myself. I reasoned that if no one else were going to do it, then I would do it myself. I was witnessing criminal behaviour and dishonesty on a daily basis in one form or another. My mum would force open the electricity or gas meter to get money. She would take a metal file to bits of tin and foreign coins and put them in the meter to get free gas or electricity.

My elder brother, Pete, who was now at sea, would often bring ornaments and carved statues home, which my mum would sell. She would take out loans and such, but there simply wasn't a lot of money about in general. The local Birkenhead Market had a second-hand shoe stall that had old shoes piled high, and it thrived. My brother, Pete, saved us from disaster a few times coming home from sea, paying rent arrears and buying food and stuff.

In the mid-1970's there was a bit of political turmoil going in Great Britain, and though at the time it was beyond my understanding it resulted in the electricity workers going on an overtime ban, and that led to blackouts throughout the country. So, each evening all the power would go off everywhere, in shops, street lighting even factories and this meant we had to use candles as it was literally pitch black. My dad had made candles from the raw chocolate from Cadbury's. It was still in an inedible form but retained the smell of chocolate, so it was particularly cruel having to smell it but being unable to eat it.

As all the shops lost power they too were reduced to using candles for light and with this came the opportunity. We descended on the shops stealing sweets using the darkness and confusion to our advantage. It was strange to be walking about with no street lights on and all the houses in darkness. I suppose it must have been like that during the war in the blackouts. Given how much we need power now it would bring the country to a standstill if it happened again, but at that time people just got on with it. We still ran around the streets in complete darkness with no thoughts to safety that is how it was.

There was one lad in the area who was a criminal through and through. He was hard as nails, and none of us would take him on. He wasn't part of our crowd but now and again would drift in and drift back out just as quickly. I think we were simply too tame for him he was involved in much bigger criminal matters than our petty pilfering. He had taken to hanging about with us again, and one day he said to a number of us come with me I've got something to show you all. I assumed it would be a dead body or a gun or a safe? He led us to a remote field and then into a little dugout den.

"Come in. Hurry up ya twats," he yelled.

We all piled inside the cramped little shelter that had been dug out of the soil and covered in old doors and plastic sheeting.

"Right," he said, "I've got some money buried here, our kid robbed, you can all have some, but if you do and he gets caught you are in the shit as well, who wants some?"

All the hands shot up, except mine!

"No, I don't want any then", I said back.

"Well fuck off then," he said, with a sneering look in his eyes. I made my way out the cramped den and walked over to the other side of the field and hid down in the grass and watched. About 20 minutes later the lads emerged, and the crook pulled branches over the den to conceal it. They all walked off. My heart was pounding. I raced to the edge of the field and watched as they all disappeared from view and then I made my way back towards the den. I scurried inside and began looking around. Nothing! He must have taken the loot with him. I searched a bit more, and in the very corner, there was some disturbed soil, so I scraped it away and found a tin. I was now shaking with both fear and excitement. I carefully opened the tin and looked inside. It was full of 50 pence pieces which were a small fortune in those days. I countered out about £5.00 put the money in my pocket put the tin back, and then I heard voices. They were outside. I was beside myself with panic. This lad would surely kill me oh I've had it I thought, I was thinking of excuses as to why I was in the den with money out the tin in my pocket. I just sat there and made no noise waiting for his head to appear but it never came, and I summoned up the courage to peek outside. There was no one there? I didn't hang about, I was gone like an Olympic athlete. I ran all the way home and made my way upstairs sweating. I took the money out my pocket and began counting it. I was rich beyond my wildest dreams.

In an instant, the bedroom door opened and my sister Ally who was a year older than me walked in her eyes falling on me with, "Wher... where did you get that?" she said.

"I'm minding it," was all I could think of.

"I'm telling," she said, about to turn around.

"No. No," I pleaded, "Come in, and I will tell you."

I told Ally the story and then offered her 50 pence for her silence.

She smirked, "I want half."

"Half?" I protested, "You didn't do anything."

"I know," she replied, "so, I won't be in trouble, so half," she repeated her demand.

I had no option. Ally took her half, but it still left me with more than enough for a sausage dinner or two and plenty over.

We often headed to the seaside resort of New Brighton which was about five miles away, so, we would travel by bus, and try and skip the fair if possible, or bunk on the train without a ticket. Even if we had the money for our fare, we would rather not pay. We hardly had money for the rides, but we would hang about looking for adventure and running wild. I remember looking at the cold drinks on hot summer days dreaming of being able to go and buy one which occasionally I did if I had the money but more often than not it was beyond my finances. One ruse we used to get money was to separate, as though we were alone, then approach an old lady and ask her the directions to Moreton as I had lost my bus fare.

Very often, the old lady would say, "Oh my, you poor little mite. It's a long, long way to walk."

Then she would fish the money out her purse and give you it, saying, "Get the bus dear."

It was a cruel con, and very wrong, but we simply didn't realise how wrong it was to us it was a game of survival, and that was that. It backfired though one day as I approached an old lady I came out with my well-rehearsed speech and a little sob for effect.

"Where are you trying to get to?" she asked me.

"Moreton Miss," I answered.

"Oh, we can't have that," she said getting her purse out her handbag.

Bingo I thought, I had in fact already spent the money mentally on a cold drink, a go on the bumper cars, or if I was really flush a go round on the Ghost Train.

"Do you know what bus to catch dear?" the old lady asked, I think, so, I replied.

Well just in case I will show you she said taking my arm.

"What?!" I thought, "shit I wasn't expecting this."

She led me to the bus stop and low and behold she saw me on to the bus paid the fare and instructed the driver to put me off in Moreton Cross and nowhere else. She waved goodbye I gave her a weak smile back, and she stepped off the bus, and it pulled away. The bus driver told me to sit at the front, which I did, and it took me home. My day didn't go to plan I was gutted and ended up on my own at home.

For one summer, one of my sisters, Lin, got a job in New Brighton Fair, working on the candy floss store. I was delighted at the prospect of free candy floss. At first, every time approached she told me to get lost and threatened to tell my mum and dad. However, a few weeks later once again down the fair trying to con old ladies, my sister beckoned me over.

"Do you want free candy floss?" she offered. It was a trap it had to be, why the change of heart?

"Yes," I replied suspiciously waiting for the trap to be sprung. No, she gave me the candy floss, and I devoured it.

"Right, come here," she said, "you can have more, but I need a favour."

"Ahh, here we go," I thought, "I knew it was too good to be true."

"Go around and get all the old candy floss sticks off the floor and out of the bins," she said, "and don't get seen and bring them back here but not if the boss is here."

The boss was an old lady, but she didn't look like the type who would give you bus fare home.

"Why do you want old sticks?" I asked puzzled.

"Never you mind," my sister said, "just get them, and you get free candy floss."

I couldn't work out what she was up to, but I was happy with the arrangement and set out to get the used candy floss sticks. I discreetly handed them over and got my reward. This arrangement lasted for the whole time she worked there, but had I have known what she was doing I would have demanded more than a few free candy flosses. It turns out the owner would put a set number of candy floss sticks in the kiosk say 400, and if she only had 100 sticks left, then she knew the till owed her 300 candy floss sales. To bypass this, my sister would wash the old sticks and sell them which were not accountable. Nice little earner for her but it was me doing all the work.

It was a good job she or I wasn't caught because the people who worked on the fairground were no fools and the penalty for causing them bother was a swift smack about the head, which I found out to my own cost one day.

The inside fair had loads of slot machines and one particular machine fascinated me. The penny shove machine always had loads of coins balancing as though ready to fall. One day I stood looking at a pile of pennies just dangling, on the edge, ready to drop into the tray and provide me with some sweets. The only problem was I didn't have a single penny to put in. So, I gave the machine a hard shove, and the pile fell, and I grabbed it out the tray not believing my luck.

"HEY, YOU LITTLE BASTARD!" I heard from across the fair, "I SAW THAT."

I looked over to see one of the staff running towards me. He looked angry, so I took off running. I was getting away, peeking over my shoulder as I ran. BANG!!! I was sitting on my arse in a daze with a bad pain in my head when I was pulled to my feet. A hand went into my pocket and removed the money I had just stolen, then I got a smack about my, already painful, head.

"Now, go on, get lost," said the man, "serves you right."

I had run straight into the glass door in my bid to escape. I staggered off with a huge lump the size of an egg on my forehead. When I arrived home, my mum was aghast.

"What the bloody hell has happened to you?" she said.

"I fell over," I lied.

"Fell over," she said, not believing me for a second but also knowing she would never get the truth anyway.

I was very envious of two lads who lived not far from me, and I would sometimes hang about with them. Their house was clean and well stocked with food. They had a phone and colour television. They also had a strip light in their kitchen which fascinated me. I had never seen one in a house, and the kitchen looked bright and clean and even had a fridge. I would always be pestering them to get me a sugar butty from their kitchen. It was basically a piece of buttered bread with sugar sprinkled on. It gave me energy much to their amusement and sometimes I would hit the jackpot and get a jam butty. These two brothers wanted for nothing and always had plenty of the luminous bright coloured fishing nets on a cane, that were popular at the time.

We would all go over to Cadbury's ponds with a milk bottle and catch the little stickleback fish. Sometimes I would see a fishing net in the pond lost by some unfortunate kid that could not retrieve it. I would make sure I did, and then I had my own fishing net. I would spend hours pursuing a net from the ponds, sometimes plunging into the water out of sheer desperation. We would go back to their house, and their mother would make them lunch, while I waited in the garden. I found this odd that their mother would make them lunch, but I was also very jealous.

"Sneak me a butty out," I would whisper.

Sometimes they did, but mostly they would tell me to go home and get my own. It's too far to walk back I would say. I was sat again waiting for them in their garden when I looked in the porch and spotted a big pile of football boots. My eyes popped out of my head! Football boots were way out of my financial reach even second-hand ones. I looked at the pile there were dozens of pairs in all styles and designs. They belonged to the brothers. As I looked harder, I spotted football shirts and shorts, socks and whole football kits just thrown in the porch. I had never worn a full football kit in my life, and I felt at that moment not just jealousy but also anger if I am honest. These two spoilt brats had that many kits they were just left in the porch. The unfairness of it was overwhelming. I felt bitterness towards them if I am truly honest and I made a plan. They came out of the house after having their lunch and washing it down with a large glass of orange juice, not just lunch but orange juice.

"Did you get me anything?" I asked.

"No," came the disappointing reply.

The lads' mother came out and told them to be careful as she was going out shopping. Perfect I thought. We set off towards Cadbury's ponds, and I said I needed to go home as I was now hungry due to them not getting me a butty. They looked puzzled as I had never gone home for food before.

They walked off saying, "See you later."

I made my way back towards their house and sat and watched. After about half an hour their mother came out the door and walked off towards the shops. My heart was beating out my chest, but I had made up my mind. I walked towards the brothers' house and rang the bell knowing I would get no answer. I walked down the alley between their house and the house next door. The back gate was locked. I jumped up and scaled over the back gate and dropped into the garden. The porch was open, and I went inside and started looking through all the football boots, trying them on. I found a pair that fit and then turned my attention to the shorts and shirts. Once I had what I wanted, I unbolted the back gate, as quietly as possible, and made my way down the entry, peeking out to make sure no one was coming.

I know now what I was doing was theft and very wrong but at that time I just thought I will never have these things, they had lots, and besides they would always get them, unlike me. I suppose that is what you do to justify to your conscience when you really know you are doing bad and it is wrong. Whatever was going through my young mind at the time, my desire to have a football kit, complete with boots, was stronger than my ability to say no.

I put the boots over my shoulder, holding them by the laces, carried the shirt and shorts, and began heading home. As I made my way past the local Morton Arms pub, it was with horror I spotted the bright glowing sight of two fishing nets being held by the two brothers. I threw the boots and kit down behind the pub wall and carried on hoping they hadn't seen me.

"Aaa!" they shouted out.

I walked over to them.

"I thought you were coming back?" one of them said.

"I was, but I thought I would knock to see if you were in first," I replied.

"You're stupid; you should have come to the ponds," one said, "we are going home now."

"Ok," I said, "see you tomorrow."

They walked off, and I retrieved my, well, their, football kit and ran home. I got changed straight away and marvelled at myself in an old cracked mirror. Like a real footballer, I thought admiring myself. I went straight out looking for a game of football, but there was unusually no one playing, and I didn't have a football myself, so, I just hung about in the kit thinking how good I looked. The two brothers never mentioned the football kit because I don't think they even noticed. Oddly neither did my parents inquire as to how I had suddenly produced a football kit out of thin air.

Some of my mates were puzzled, and I told them, but their reaction was "Can I get some?"

It was how the world worked in our lives if there was an opportunity, even a criminal opportunity, you didn't turn it down because you never knew if you would get that chance again.

My mother's drinking was now tearing her and us apart. It was now at a level where it simply couldn't be ignored by anyone, yet somehow my father carried on. I am not sure how he was able to do this, but he did. But the house and all our lives were really deeply affected each and every moment. On the days we did attend school, I dreaded coming in the door because I wouldn't know what mood she would be in. If she had managed to find alcohol, she would possibly be asleep in the chair or near unconscious if the truth were known. Had she been unable to get alcohol then the situation was, for me at least, far worse because she would be in a very foul mood and shouting and somehow blaming us for her situation.

I wanted so many times to shout back, "WHY IS IT OUR FUCKING FAULT? WHY?"

But I couldn't so I would just bite my tongue and say to myself, "I haven't done anything to deserve this, so, get lost."

I would go into the kitchen and look at the empty cold stove, with nothing cooking on it, and say to myself, "Oh, what's for dinner tonight the same as last night?"

I would go in the cupboard and be told, "Don't touch that milk there is only enough for your dad."

"Why is there only ever enough for my dad?" I would question myself and mimic the answer, "Because you haven't bought any, AGAIN."

I would then be told, "Don't touch those two slices of bread, there's only enough for your dad."

That was the mantra we lived by, "There's only enough for your dad."

"It must be good to be me dad," I thought, "there always enough if it's him."

My bitterness I think was borne out of lack of anything. Food, clothing, normal household items and normality, there was no normality or continuity of happiness, it came now and again but was all too brief to embrace it and get to know it. I had no trust in anything, not my family, in my school or adults. Adults told lies and let you down. People made promises that they never kept or had any intention of keeping. I was disappointed with the world. It wasn't a utopia for me. It was one long existence of nothing very pleasant.

There was nothing that made me say, "Wow, isn't life great! I am having a super time."

It just wasn't like that I was always waiting for the next disappointment, the next let down. I would go out in the street to see the lad down the road on his new bike because it was his birthday. I never got a birthday card, and they got bikes.

"So, why was this?" I would ask myself.

I knew the answer deep down I suppose. My mother's drinking and my father's utter selfishness in only taking care of himself. Don't get me wrong it pains me, but it is the truth. He would never consider buying us school clothes, which would have drastically reduced the bullying and made our lives so much better, let alone buy us luxury items such as bikes. I don't recall him once encouraging me or telling me I was any good at anything. I, therefore, dismissed him as a father in the sense he was a dad. We said nothing to each other except when he was telling me off for some reason.

The grim reality was that we as children looked after ourselves and made our own opportunities it was survival. Day to day chores had their dangers just going to the shop was a task, as Berrylands Road, where I lived, was a long horseshoe shaped road and different gangs had their own patch and to get to the shops on an errand, you had to pass through their territory. One gang had an older lad who would lead the rest, and he was always out and waiting. His feet used to point in the direction of ten minutes to two if they were the hands of a clock. I was fascinated by them and surprised he didn't sweep litter up as he walked. His oddly pointed feet sadly didn't slow him down when he was chasing you for daring to walk past his house though. It was tiresome because I would have no option sometimes, rather like a thirsty wildebeest that has to approach a pond knowing the crocodile is waiting, well that was him and me, or anyone who wasn't in his gang. If there were equal numbers, he and his cronies would just shout. Sometimes my mother would send me to pick up a bag of Trend which was little sacks of coal in plastic bags you threw straight on the fire. I was six stone at most so putting the coal on my shoulder and having a sole hanging off my shoe while being pursued by '10 to 2 feet' was hard work. My shoulder would be black and blue with bruising by the time I got home.

Years later, when I was in the army doing a parachute selection course, we had to run with metal tubes filled with concrete and metal struts across, which they described as a stretcher, it wasn't, it was a torture device. While running on that para course, my shoulder was being battered by the metal poles, and I truly had a flashback to being chased by '10 to 2 feet', down Berrylands Road, with a bag of Trend Coal on my shoulder.

One day, as I approached enemy turf, '10 to 2 feet' was, as usual, waiting, I wasn't sure if he didn't sleep outside. I decided to change my tack and walked straight up to him. He looked nervous and a little surprised that I was going to him and alone! This guy liked a particular pop group, and I stopped in front of him and asked his advice on the lyrics of one of their songs. His scowl softened, and he began giving me the entire lyrics. I thanked him and praised him for his outstanding knowledge and went on my way to the shop. On the way back he waved, and I learned that sometimes talk is better than running and a lot better than getting caught.

Sadly, not all the hostiles could be softened up with talk. One particular day I was, to say the least, ravenous with hunger and I had to address it by hook or by crook. A rummage of the house proved fruitless apart from a stale piece of bread which I put under the tap to soften up, but it was beyond even saving with a wash. A very old glass jar that had some kind of Gherkins in also proved inedible on opening the lid; they had to be fair been on the shelve in the empty pantry as long as I could remember. There was not even an opportunity to steal from anywhere, so I was feeling weak and sorry for myself. I didn't even have the energy to looking for the rest of my mates and raiding Cadbury's was out of the question during day light and working hours.

I was at a loss, so I decided to go knocking on doors to see if any of the neighbours needed any errands or they had any old lemonade bottles I could take back and get the recycling fee back. I was having no luck until the last, but one house and I was about to give up but decided to knock anyway. I was in luck the lady came to the door with a stack of lemonade bottles! Yes, I was thrilled. I struggled to pick them up and seeing my plight she gave me an old bag. I put them all in some just hanging over the side. It was a great bounty, and I set off, but within minutes one of the bottles toppled out and smashed I was gutted but made sure the rest were going nowhere. I had made up my mind it was the chippy when I got paid out. Steak and kidney pie! That's what I will get I thought my belly is rumbling.

I got to the shops and began handing the bottles in. Mrs Bartlett who ran one of the shops scrutinised the bottles for her signature through her glasses like a detective looking at finger prints. She resembled the actress Maggie Smith. Every now and again she would look up at me suspiciously as though I was trying to pass counterfeit money.

"These two are mine," she said putting the few coins on the counter, "those are NOT!"

I put my dirty hand on the counter to scoop up my profits when she grabbed my hand.

"Remember, Father Time gets us all," she said.

"Oh right," I said, not having a clue what she was on about, my concern was my belly and the pie next door, though that was still out of reach until I cashed in my other two bottles.

I ran across the road to another shop run by a very kind woman Mrs Gough. She inspected the bottles and accepted they were hers, and the signatures were not forgeries, though they had good reason because we would often forge their signatures if we had bottles from somewhere far or without any signatures.

I had enough money for my pie and went straight to the chippy.

"Steak and kidney pie," I said to the Chinese women.

"The money," she demanded holding out her hands, not trusting me one inch.

I got my pie and made my way home feeling even more starving after my efforts. As I walked down Berrylands Road, I unwrapped it and the intense smell of hit my nose. I took a bite, and although it was delicious, it was hot, so, I held it making sure none of the precious gravy spilt out. WOOFFFF! In an instant, the pie was out my hand and being devoured by a black and clearly overweight and greedy bastard dog. I went to try and grab it back from its mouth, and it curled its lips back showing its teeth and growling menacingly with an 'It's you or the pie' look in its eyes. It dropped the pie on the floor, splitting it open, then it began eating it and licking the gravy off the pavement. It finished it, my pie, wagged its tail and went off down a nearby alleyway between two houses.

I stood there, not believing what had just happened, as my sorrow turned to anger.

"My fucking pie," I cried to no one.

"Bastard!" I yelled down the alleyway.

"That dog is not getting away with it," I thought.

I made my way home almost crying.

"Right, you greedy bastard," I thought, "payback."

I waited till later that day and asked one of my mates for a couple of butties. I ate one and then got the other slice, that was covered in margarine. I went home and emptied the entire contents of a white pepper pot on to the bread and folded it in two. I didn't like wasting a piece of bread, but I had been done over by that dog good and proper as they say.

I made my way back up the road, and when I neared the dog's house, I made sure I was pretending to eat the bread. On cue, the dog seeing another easy meal ran towards me, so, I threw the bread. It began woofing it down and within seconds let out an ear splitting long howl. Then it began coughing, and croaking, and then howling. Front doors began to open, and people came out to see what the noise was.

"Is that dogs fighting?" someone shouted.

"I think a dog's been hit by a car," some replied.

The pie thief was now down the alleyway, still screaming, and running at what sounded like the gate where its bowl of water must have been. I headed back home and ran in to the garden but I could still hear the dog.

"Ha! Ha! Revenge," I thought, "serves you right."

I think at this time, in the 1970's, money was tight everywhere and there wasn't so much extravagance as we see now. People had to save for things, get clothes and such, from catalogues, and save for things like new jeans and such. But some people simply had little choice of saving; there was no money to save.

Once a garden with a washing line full of clothes had been spotted, we would jump over the fence and help ourselves to the best of the items. Once we had our booty, we would head home, and some of my sisters and their friends would sort out what they wanted.

One night I did a solo raid on a washing line where there were a couple of pairs of trendy jeans. I hopped over our garden fence and headed a short distance down the railway line to the garden and waited in the shadows to see if there was anyone about. It was freezing, and I decided to go for it rather than wait any longer. I climbed over the fence and slowly made my way up the garden. I grabbed the first pair of jeans, but they were frozen solid. I folded them over, and it sounded and felt like bending cardboard.

I was about to move on to the second pair when a light went on in the kitchen of the house illuminating the garden in a pool of light including me. I froze as solid as the jeans on the ground next to me and instinctively moved into the small bushes in the garden border not daring to move.

"I'm caught," I thought, "no question."

A woman appeared and saw the jeans lying on the ground. She turned around and shouted into the house, and her husband emerged.

"Some bastard has been in the garden," he hissed, walking over to the jeans and picking them up.

He told his wife to get the rest of the clothes off the line, and he looked about, even towards my direction. I had my mouth inside my coat trying not to breathe tell tail vapours of hot breath into the freezing night air. He told his wife to get his torch. I really knew the game was up; this hero is now going to start looking around, then he is going find me and then I am going to get a good thumping.

"You've got your jeans still, you bastard," I thought.

The wife appeared again.

"I can't find it," she said.

"It's in the second draw in the kitchen," he said, then adding, "the bastards will be long gone."

I almost wanted to shout, yes, long gone, now go in. The wife came out with his torch, and he made his way to the end of the garden.

"No nothing here!" he shouted back to his wife.

"Okay come on in love," she shouted, "it's freezing."

She was right I had been crouching for what seemed like an eternity, my legs were numb and I very cold. It was only a matter of time before I would have to stand up such was the agony. Eventually, he made his way back up the garden to his wife.

"I know which thieving bastard that will be," he said to his wife and then named one of the lads in our gang.

If I hadn't been so scared, I would have burst out laughing.

He went into the house with his wife and the light went off. I stayed perfectly still just in case. My instincts were right because as my eyes adjusted, I could just make him out still outside by the kitchen door watching. Then I heard him shuffle and the kitchen light went back on, and I saw him head towards the living room. Time to go. I got up and began running towards the back fence, but my legs had seized due to the crouching and cold, and I had to make every effort to keep going. I jumped over the fence and my flared pants, which were fashionable at the time, caught on the fence ripping and sending me tumbling into the brambles. I was cut to ribbons and staggered on to the track and headed home. What a disaster. No jeans torn pants and cuts and scratches with a dose of hypothermia. Line robbing and I were finished, there had to be something easier than this.

I now had the problem of needing new trousers, and I knew that problem wasn't going to be solved by anyone but me.

We had a men's clothing store in Moreton Cross, and they sold 'Birmingham Bags', which were bell bottomed trousers and the height of fashion. The man who owned the store was a bit strict looking, but one of the lads had flannelled him a few weeks earlier by taking numerous pairs of pants into the changing room and keeping a pair on under his own crap pants. If he hadn't caught on to it, I decided I would have a go. As I opened the door, he gave a warm, welcoming smile and then looked me up and down. He didn't try to hide his disappointment at the smelly urchin in front of him, who he knew didn't have a single penny and therefore no prospect of a sale. With that knowledge, he was unlikely to give me the opportunity to try on his wares. However, I had a plan to subdue his accurate opinion of me.

"Me mum has told me to come and look for some new pants, and she is going to buy them on Thursday," I lied.

"Oh okay," he replied, now sensing he may get a sale out of the urchin after all.

"What are you after?" He said with enthusiasm.

"Birmingham Bags," I replied.

After going through the colours and such, he gave me a few pairs, and I asked for a couple more and retreated to the changing rooms. I had about five pairs, and I picked out a brown pair I was going to steal. I hurriedly put them on and pulled my own pair over the top tucking the bottoms in my socks so he wouldn't see them. I was checking myself in the mirror when he shouted through the curtains

"What colours do you have in there?"

I shouted back all the colours but omitted the brown ones which I now had on underneath my own pants.

"AND THE BROWN PAIR!" he shouted back with authority.

"Oh, yeah, sorry, they're here on the bench," I replied while stripping my pants off to get the brown pair off fast.

I came out of the changing room, and he counted the pants.

"Which pair do like then?" he enquired.

"I am not sure," I said, "I will come back in with me mum."

The game was already up with that little scam, he must have realised he had lost a pair and figured it out.

I now moved to my senior school, and with age, bigger and better opportunities came, though sadly not in my attendance as I was only there a few weeks and the same pattern of not bothering to go into school emerged. Even when I did go in most of the subjects had moved on so far that I was out of step anyway and it was pointless.

I recall a very caring and good English teacher sitting me down and saying, "Why?"

"Why what?" I replied baffled.

"Why don't you come into school?" he went on, "It seems like you enjoy it and if you knuckle down, you would be way ahead of most of those who are here every single day."

I had no answer for him, and he looked disappointed. By now I was only interested in one thing, and that was leaving home the moment I left school.

My every waking thought was to get away from my house and the constant misery of my mother's drinking and the grim atmosphere of despair I felt. There was no soap, no towels no nothing but an endless cycle of mood swings and rows over money. My mother in her world my father in his world and us just floating about somewhere in between.

My dad would sit and hog the telly now we finally had one on a permanent basis. Even if we were just sitting watching a film and it was near the end, he would switch over to what he wanted to watch without any hesitation, and any protest would be met with a shout. I don't think it really even entered his head such was his selfishness. Saturdays would see him sitting watching the horse racing. The living room would be blanketed in a very thick fog of blue cigarette smoke from him and my mother puffing away. I was fascinated by the shafts of sunlight as they penetrated the smoke in the living room. Everything was tinged in nicotine giving the room the appearance that it had been painted in pale orange. My dad would sit looking intently at the screen willing his horse on as though it was him riding it he would get closer to the screen making the movements of a jockey on the chair. As the horse inevitably let him down, he would swear to calm down and then cough at the exertion of having just ridden his imaginary hose a couple of furlongs around the course. Then he would roll another cigarette pick up his next bet, and the whole process would start again.

Sometimes I would use the opportunity to ask for money if he was successful. He would look at me surprised at my audacity.

"What, do you think I am made of money?" he would reply.

Betting over he would then say to my mother, "I'm off for a pint," and then he was gone to the Morton Arms pub whose bar staff must have thought he was made of money.

The Morton Arms pub was my dad's oasis, his watering hole his social club, his second home. I used to be baffled as to why it was spelt 'Morton' instead of 'Moreton'. It turns out that it was because they could only find a coat of arms for Morton and not Moreton!

It was a typical pub of that era. Its purpose to serve the people on the surrounding council estates. It had, as most pubs, a bar for the men and a 'best end' as it was known, to go when dressing nice and looking for a bit more class, such as carpet on the floor and padded seats.

When the bar was full, it would be mostly men from the older generation who fought in the war, to the up and coming young lads who were just moving into adulthood and all it can offer. Sometimes while waiting for my dad while on a money borrowing errand for my mother, I would wait inside by the door but out of sight of the bar staff. As a young lad, it seemed quite aggressive the way the men shouted and swore at each other. The ubiquitous blue cloud of cigarette smoke hung over the people like a giant blanket. Men heaved and coughed phlegm from their obviously diseased lungs. They would spit flecks of tobacco in all directions and then start glugging on their beer. Old men would be coming out of the toilet still heaving their genitals into a more comfortable position while farting at the same time. They all seemed to be wearing trousers with suit jackets that didn't match and were shiny with wear. They all had braces on, and lots had caps still on despite being indoors. Men played darts and argued with each other swearing and squaring up. I couldn't work out why my dad would want to come in here; it was like a Wild West saloon to me. After his afternoon session, he would come home and have some dinner and fall asleep in the chair in front of the telly, shoes off. His tobacco tin and lighter with the paper open on the racing page on the table in front of him.

"I know where there are some pigeons," I said to my mate who had a passion for them and kept a loft in his back garden.

It was a dull Sunday afternoon, so we decided to take a stroll to the small bridge at the end of a nearby motorway. I had seen them going under there. We arrived at the bridge and went underneath to have a look, and sure enough, the pigeons were there roosting and flying in and out. The only problem was that it was too high to get at them from the ground and the smooth concrete wall offered no chance of climbing up.

"We are not going to be able to get them," my mate said disappointedly.

Too be honest I am not sure what we hoped to do anyway, but that wasn't the point. We sat looking at the pigeons in frustration and then I had an idea!

"What if we go on top of the motorway bridge and I hold you by the legs, and you reach down and see if you can see anything," I suggested.

He was the pigeon expert so there was no point in him holding me, besides he might drop me! To my surprise, he readily agreed. We made our way back up to the top of the bridge, and my mate climbed over the rail guard. He lay on the small ledge, and I grabbed his ankles while he slowly lowered his body over the edge. He was a dead weight to my small frame, but I held on as tight as I could.

"Can you see anything?" I shouted to him.

"Yes," he replied enthusiastically, "there's some in here."

"Can you reach them?" I shouted back.

"Yes," came the faint reply as he wriggled for a better look.

As he moved position, his weight seemed to increase, and then he was gone! I looked at my empty hands to be sure my mind wasn't playing tricks but no they were definitely empty. The moaning coming from below confirmed my suspicions, I had, in fact, dropped the poor bastard. I ran down to where he had landed shouting apologies but also putting the blame on him for wriggling about. He had landed on grass otherwise he wouldn't have been alive.

"Sorry mate," I kept repeating, "Are you alright?"

"No," he moaned, "I've hurt me arm."

He looked white. I looked at his arm, and it was hanging at a funny angle. I helped him up, and we used his coat as a sling to support the clearly broken arm. I managed to get him back up the bank but he was in pain, so we decided to knock on the door of the first house we came to. These were what we considered posh given that they were private and not council like ours. I tapped on the door of the first house, and after a few seconds a woman came and opened the door.

On seeing the two of us, who were not dressed in our Sunday best, on account that we didn't have one, she looked us up and down and said in a very snooty voice, "What do you want?"

I explained that my friend who by now had tears in his eyes with the pain had fallen and broken his arm.

The lady pulled a grimacing face and then said, "GO AWAY AND DON'T KNOCK HERE AGAIN!" in a loud voice and then she slammed the door.

We trudged off back up the path and walked back to Moreton. On reaching the ambulance station, we rang the bell but there was no answer, so we sat and waited. By now my mate was all but ready to drop, but luckily the ambulance arrived, and we stood up to greet them.

"What's up lads?" they said in a cheery voice.

My mate showed them his arm, and they immediately packed him into the ambulance and took him away. I was given the job of going home to tell his mum and dad.

For some time, my older brother, Boe, had left his old, Honda 70, motorbike abandoned on the front lawn of our house. I had, had my eye on it for a long while, and one day I decided, as he had moved out, to claim what I considered was rightly mine. After spending a few days putting the front wheel back on the engine refused to start. My mates and I were at a loss as to why we couldn't get it going.

One day, however, my elder sister Sue's boyfriend Geoff, who knew his way around mechanics, took a look at it and got it going. It had no exhaust and flames shot out the bottom, but it was okay by me. I was dancing with joy. We all chipped in for petrol and headed off to the old tip field behind our house.

The area was quite big and had once been the tip, but it had now been filled in and grassed over with a small hill on one end, and the grass was long but okay to ride through. The motorbike gave us days of endless entertainment, and I didn't mind sharing it with the rest of the gang and we would all take turns riding across the field and shooting up the hill faster than we should. Though we were not on the road, it was still a public area though deserted and we had to keep an eye out for the police. If they did turn up, we would speed off to the other side of the field where their cars couldn't follow us and once they had gone carry on with the fun.

It was Stewy Martindale's turn on the bike, and we watched as he zoomed around the field with a look of joy on his face. We waved at him across the field to let him know it was someone else's turn. He waved back to let us know he had seen us and turned towards us and the hill, however, as he got closer, he gained speed instead of reducing it. His clothes and hair looked like he was in a wind tunnel and he had a look of determination on his face. Once he hit the bottom of the hill without slowing, I knew it wasn't going to end well. We all sat open mouthed as he whizzed past now frantically pumping the foot brake. It was futile as the bike had now gathered up so much speed it had left the ground and he was flying through the air. He passed us with a whoosh of air and a look of resignation on his face that he was going to be hurt and soon. He disappeared out of view over the hill, and there was an enormous bang and the sound of scraping and the engine screaming, but no sound from him.

We all raced over to see him lying some way from the bike which had now stopped on the kerb of the small service road. I was horrified at the prospect of his injuries and the trouble I would be in. To my utter disbelief, he began to get to his feet and started telling us the brakes had failed!

"You fucking idiot!" I screamed, "The brakes didn't work because you had left the ground."

"Did I?" he said, pleased with his achievement.

"You twat. You ain't going on it again," I told him.

"I am," he replied, "you all enjoyed that."

The bike was bashed but still ridable. Like he knew I would, I relented and let him on it again, but once again he had to break the rules. He had been on it ages and wouldn't come back to let someone else have a go. He kept coming closer and shouting obscenities to no one, in particular, laughing to himself at our attempts to chase him.

He had been doing this for a while when I said, "Don't chase him, that's what he wants. Let him get closer."

He fell for it and began riding past closer and closer pulling faces and laughing. As he drew close, on one run, I pulled a huge stone from behind my back and launched it at him. It hit him bang on his hand, and he let go of the handle bars to grab his painful injured hand and went arse over tit, hitting the ground with a thud, for the second time that day. I don't know what his pain threshold was, but he was up again trying to get the bike started before we finally got it from him.

This time it was my turn, so I decided to have a big go as it was my bike anyway. With the gang was Half-wit, who I had slammed the door on in the woman's house and he had not been happy. He asked if he could get on the back, so I let him. We were riding around for ages when one of the hardest lads in the gang began getting frustrated as it was his turn for a go. He was hard but not a bully and would only thump you if you provoked him which we often did and then we would beg for mercy.

"Give me a go. It's my turn!" he shouted, as we flew past.

"Fuck off," we laughed trying to get him fired up.

He made a few attempts at chasing us, and we rode just enough away until he tried again and then sped off. He was now angry!

As we did another pass, I said to Half-wit, "Get off and walk towards him, call him names and then when he chases you run to the bike, and we will ride off."

So, I stopped just the right distance away, and Half-wit climbed off.

"You big knob!" he shouted, "Come and have a go!"

The lad was up and running, and Half-wit turned towards me on the bike and began running towards me, and I rode off. On looking back, I could see a mixture of confusion and fear on Half-wit's face as the lad gained on him. He was on him like a lion on a zebra and began clouting him. I never once considered what I had done as cruel. That's just how it was.

I loved being out of the house and roaming about enjoying myself and getting up to mischief. Even though some of our exploits were bordering on or were indeed criminal, I think the time and circumstances had a lot to do with it. I don't believe that it occurred to us that some of the stuff was not just against the law it was also morally wrong.

We would readily steal milk from door steps or in the summer some people had orange delivered by the milkman, in bottles much like the milk. After running about in the hot sun and spotting it, there was simply no question of us not having it away. If there were a chance to get fed or watered I would seize it with both hands no question. I had never been in a restaurant or had any posh meals. I had never been further than South Shields where my elder sister, Jean, lived, or Barrow in Furness, where my father was from.

I remember my brother Pete coming home from sea, and he had been to places like Singapore and Australia. I couldn't even imagine what those places were like, let alone have any real ambition of actually seeing them. When I was little, he would bring me gifts home, of Thunderbirds, Batman figures and Scalextric racing car sets, which were still not out in production in the UK. My brother, Pete, was a beacon of light in a somewhat dark world in those days and I will always be grateful to him. We had a programme when I was younger called Skippy, I was amazed that he had been to the same place. I was unaware of just how big Australia was. The most exotic fayre I had eaten was from the Chinese chippy.

My sister, Sue, would come home from a night out with Geoff, her boyfriend, they would each have a Chinese meal and my two sisters, and I would put in our bid and ask for any leftovers, meaning if they couldn't eat it all could we have what was left. We would sit at their feet while they tucked in waiting and if I am honest praying, they couldn't manage it all. It is only now I wonder, given they knew we were hungry, why they didn't bother to pick up a bag of chips with their meal, but they didn't. It never crossed my own mind at the time why they didn't, but I suppose it says more about their own minds at the time than ours. My parents would also sit unfazed by our begging, and that is what it was begging, begging for food. Sitting and waiting for leftovers.

Inevitably as we grew older, we sought better adventures, and our minds looked for better things. I managed to get hold of an air rifle, and I liked it a lot I started off shooting cardboard targets and very quickly grew bored and moved on to people. One day I was at the bottom of our garden when I spotted '10 to 2 feet' over the railway line on the quarry. I remembered all the times he had chased me, so the gloves were off. I fired a pellet right next to him, and it actually ricocheted like on the cowboy films with a ping and a whizz. On hearing, it and seeing it so close, '10 to 2 feet' spun around to see me aiming my rifle at him.

"Fuck off!" he protested.

"No, you fuck off," I answered firing another shot but closer.

"Try and run!" I shouted reading his mind.

He stood there shaking, and I loved it.

"I'm going to shoot you up the arse," I teased.

"Why we're mates?" '10 to 2 feet' replied.

"No, we're not. Now do me a little dance, and I won't shoot you!" I shouted at him.

"I don't know how to dance!" he shouted back.

"Just do a little jig but do something," I mocked him.

"I can feel another pellet coming your way," I warned.

"WHAT ARE YOU DOING YOU LITTLE IDIOT?" Someone shouted at me.

It was the girl next door.

"Nothing," I replied just firing at targets.

"No, you're not," she retorted, "you're shooting at that poor lad."

I turned to get '10 to 2 feet' to tell her I wasn't but he had gone in a cloud of dust.

"And while we are at it," she said, "if you shoot any more holes in my underwear on the washing line you've had it."

I was genuinely puzzled at this because I hadn't fired at her washing. It was only years later I found out my two brothers had turned her knickers into Swiss cheese and I got the blame. I decide to move back to target practice in the garden.

As I was firing at bits of cardboard and the odd peg off our washing line, a bird flew over and without a moment's thought I lifted the rifle and fired in its direction. There was a crack, and a slap and the bird nosedived into the garden with a thud! I stood completed shocked that I had hit it and then I was overwhelmed by remorse. It hit me like a train. I had just killed the little bird going about its business on a beautiful summer's day. I felt sick with grief. I walked over to see the little sparrow lying there dead with blood on its chest eyes still open.

"Oh no, what have I done," I thought to myself.

I never thought for one second I would have hit it, but I had. It was strange because I was happy to torment '10 to 2 feet' but this affected me. I dug a hole and put the bird in an old sock and buried it. I stood looking at its grave and questioned my own guilt at what I had done. I asked myself how sorry I was, was I really sorry or was I just going through the motions? I decided there and then. I went into my dad's shed put my rifle in the vice and got a saw and cut the gun barrel off, and the butt, and threw it in the bin. I never told my mates about this because I didn't want to appear soft and have them laugh at me.

Later on, in my life when I became a soldier I was in the Falklands War, and I remember firing my rifle up at the Argentine aircraft which were attacking us, and I had thought back to that day. The fundamental difference was evident, but I still had that feeling of trying to take life. Later on, that day I made a comparison in my mind. It was wrong to kill that innocent little bird but was it wrong to try and kill human beings who were trying to kill you? The answer seems obvious, and it is no, but how strange that sometimes it's okay if we are not friends and in time when we become friends it's not okay. Really it is only other people who are making that decision for you, namely, politicians. A greedy bunch of self-serving hypocrites, make decisions, of such magnitude, that decide on who lives and dies and change so many people's lives forever, even though they move on, and retire, without another thought to what they have done. I guess that is how it is and always has been.

As a gang of friends living in Moreton, we all began to want more adult entertainment, girls, beer, going to the cinema, and such. One or two found girlfriends, bought their own motorbikes and started taking an interest in their appearance. I had a drawback in that I was still tiny and looked very much like a kid. When some of the lads began to get some facial hair, and their voices began to deepen, I was still talking in a falsetto voice. Getting into a pub was out of the question for me at least.

We once all decided to go to the cinema to watch an 18-rated film or an X-rated film as it was known. It wasn't anything rude or such and would probably be seen on normal telly these days, but I guess it was still strict that way in the 1970's. One or two of us needed help to try and look older if we stood any chance of getting in to watch a big boys film. I borrowed a pair of platform shoes which were in fashion. They were two sizes too big, and I put toilet paper down the toes because every time I took a step, I would slide to the front. I had trouble walking in them because of the height and weight. I combed my hair into what I considered an adult fashion. Then the thing I thought we would transform me into a man, women's mascara. I began applying this to the very few and thin little white hairs on the top of my lip; a strong wind would have blown them away. I applied the mascara liberally and checked myself out in the mirror. I looked okay, I thought. Black platform shoes, cream flared trousers and a checked jacket that was a little big in the sleeves and my moustache.

We all made our way to the bus stop, and I noticed some people looking and giggling. I thought I looked a million dollars and winked at some girl at the bus stop. I could tell she liked me because she stood staring with her mouth open. As the bus pulled in, I suddenly realised I would need an adult ticket on account that I was now a man.

"One adult to Seacome, mate," I said to the driver in my best man's voice.

"It's okay you can still get a child's fare when you're in fancy dress," he laughed and laughed and laughed.

We walked down the bus much to the amusement of all the passengers. I could still hear the driver laughing. I sat feeling confident despite the giggles rippling through the bus and people turning to get another look. As the bus pulled up at one stop a couple of older lads got on and immediately started laughing when they saw us. They purposely sat right by us knowing they could amuse themselves on the journey.

"What the fuck you dressed like that for?" one of them said to me.

"Like what?" I said trying to sound hard.

"Like a little man, you little boy."

"It's how I always dress" I replied.

"Where are you going?" he teased.

"To the cinema," I said blushing.

"Oh, I see," he said, realising what we were doing.

"You're all going to try and get in to watch a rudie film, aren't you? Tut-tut," he mocked, wagging his finger, "You are naughty boys."

"We're not," I protested, "it's just a film."

"Yes, but is it an X-rated or somewhat?" he mocked further.

"Yes, I replied, why?"

"Oh, because I was wondering why you have drawn a moustache on your lip," he said laughing.

Much to my relief the older boys got off at the next stop but not before sharing a joke with the driver, which I guessed might be about us.

The bus arrived at the cinema, and we all piled off. I was a little less confident now after my mocking but reasoned I had come this far so I might as well try. We waited outside for more people to arrive so the staff would be busy and might not pay us too much attention. We piled in on the end of the line, and I grew more nervous as we got closer to the kiosk to get our ticket. The first of our gang got through, and it was my turn.

"Same love," I said to the woman, who was looking down as she went to issue the ticket and looked up at me.

"You can't watch that," she said.

"Why?" I replied.

"Because it's an 18 and you are not 18 years old," she said, now smirking.

"I am 18," I lied.

"You are not, and you have drawn a pretend moustache on your lip, and those are not your clothes," she said, "now go and play."

I tried to protest, but she was having none of it. I walked out totally dejected, feeling sorry for myself, all the others had got in! I rubbed the moustache off, took the jacket off and ruffled my hair to lose the centre parting that I thought had added years to my appearance. It seemed like I had a while to go before there was any chance of me getting to see the adult world.

Around this time my friends and people at school were now considering what they would do for a job. No one even considered University, a trip to the moon was more likely. Given I had not attended, I, therefore, wasn't even considered as a serious candidate to take any exams and one teacher told me so.

"The sooner you leave and start your prison career the better," he said, "You are a complete and utter waste of time."

His stinging remarks, however, did set my mind thinking about my prospects but the truth was I had already made up my mind to leave home one way or another. I was always interested in travelling to see the world, even at that time my geography wasn't great, I wanted to see the places my brother had been to and spoken of. I didn't have a plan of how I was going to see these places but I was, one way or another, I knew that I would. My thinking was correct because, by the time I was 40 years old, I had stood on all the continents. I made the odd appearance in school and then just stopped altogether, I didn't see the point.

There was a knock on the door, and I opened it to see one of my friends standing there.

"You've left school," he said smiling.

"I know," I replied, "I don't need you to tell me."

"No, you don't understand," he said, "the teacher told me to tell you you've really left, even though you haven't been in for months anyway."

"Thanks," I said.

That was it, that was all I was waiting for, now my destiny was in my own hands. It was up to me what I did with my life from here on in. No one could decide for me anymore. I felt a little nervous but also relief that I could now head in any direction I wanted, so I decided to head south. I boarded the train from Liverpool to London with a little bag with all my possessions in it which wasn't much.

My sister, Doris, had met a man called Don, who originally came from Cumbria but was living in London. They had moved into an apartment, in Collier Row, in Essex. Don was a larger than life character, who had served in the Scots Guards, and he was as hard as nails but one of the nicest men I have ever met. After working as a rep for a petrol company chain which was how he met my sister, he was now doing bit and bobs or to be more accurate ducking and diving and had a finger in every pie in and around London. Being young and naïve I had no idea to what level of involvement he had and in what but I think to be honest it wasn't all entirely innocent.

Don met me at London's Euston station, and we drove in his Mercedes Bentley to Collier Row.

"You need bloody feeding up," he said looking at me.

"I know," I agreed.

We arrived at the apartment and went in. I was astounded. It was the height of luxury! Thick carpets on the floor, beautiful sofas and décor, even America style telephones in colours that I had never seen at the time. They showed me to my room, and it was modern, clean and decorated all nice with a bed and pillows, pillows what a luxury. When they showed me the bathroom, I was taken aback. It had a coloured bathroom suite, carpet, shower tiles, towels, toothpaste and soap. To me it was like stepping into a world I had only seen on the telly, I never knew that such luxury was real.

"Unpack, and then you can come down for dinner," Don said.

I sat on the bed and felt very emotional. The bed was clean and fresh with sheets. I went down stairs for dinner, and it was a curry which I had never had apart from the Vesta dehydrated packs that people ate in the 70's before Indian restaurants came to the Wirral. I had no idea what the large pieces of white bread were that were on the plate next to my curry.

"Tuck in," Don urged, "eat your Pitta bread."

"Pitta bread?" I thought, "what is that?"

He read my mind.

"Try it," he said, pointing at the bread.

I did and couldn't believe how nice it all was, the curry, my surroundings, everything. But I had a nagging doubt, it can't be real there has got to be a catch I thought. I didn't trust it all. It was in my mind too good to be true. And that distrust of life is still with me, it is one of the residual elements of my life, I have never been able to shake off.

Don had bought a house for him and my sister, Doris, in Goodmayes and it was in serious need of renovation. They charged me no rent, so, I would help him. How, was still a little confusing, because I lacked even the most basic building skills and struggled to lift a bag of sugar let alone a bag of cement?

After dinner, Don invited me to go take a bath. I wasn't used to baths but took up the offer of trying their posh bath. Strangely enough, they even had a spare toothbrush. I hadn't twigged on that it was all worked out before hand and I was more than happy to embark on a journey of keeping myself clean that is with me forever.

The following Monday, we drove over to Goodmayes, near Ilford, to the Semi-detached house, Don had bought.

"Are you ready for this?" he asked, as we drew up the drive.

"Yes?" I replied, puzzled.

Once we got inside, I quickly realised this was no short make-over, this was a major refurbishment. When we first started, I had trouble even lifting a bag of cement and carrying some of the tools. Don gave no quarter and insisted that I just keep going until I could do it. I had never used power tools, but he once again insisted that I had to learn. He slowly built up my confidence and strength, and I am grateful to him for that.

I settled in well in London, and I become more aware of my own social short comings. I never had drunk wine or been out to dinner, but I began to do all these things and more besides. I missed having mates around me, but I didn't miss the circumstances of living at home one single bit. I bought new clothes and smartened up my appearance. I began looking forward to driving over to the house we were renovating, and I also began to fill out with the good diet and physical work. Don had a good sense of humour, and as time went on I realised just how funny he was, but that funny side also hid a man who knew how to look after himself. Don was very hard indeed but a gentleman none the less, and you knew where you stood with him.

One day, as we worked on the house, there was a knock on the door, and I answered it. There were two scruffy looking men standing there.

"Hello boy," they greeted.

"Your drive?"

"No, I don't drive," I replied.

"No, listen here. Drive, boy."

I was now puzzled.

"No, I haven't driven," I said thinking they were mad men.

They began to giggle, "No, you daft little fucker yee, dat you drive?"

I looked over his shoulder at the car, "No. I haven't driven it."

Were they accusing me of driving?

"Git ya daddy," one of them piped up.

"Don!" I shouted.

Don came to the door.

"What?" he said without any politeness.

"Yeh sons a little thick, 'A', goes to the daft school?" one of the men said to Don.

I could see Don ready to show them out the front garden.

"Look we have da tarmac, what about if we put it down for ya nice and cheap?" one of the men said.

The front was a mess and full of potholes, so, Don reasoned it would help for now getting materials delivered and such.

They bartered for a while and agreed on an amount of cash and one of the old cars that were on the front. Don stipulated he wanted the tarmac to have red stone in it, to at least make it look presentable, if only for a while until he had the drive done again in stone. They shook hands, then Don had to go off to do some business in London and told me to keep an eye on them, warning me not to let them in the house. I wondered how I could watch them when I couldn't even understand their broad Irish accents. None the less I watched as they threw the tarmac down while shouting at each other. I sat on the step and watched in delight at the arguments. One of them turned to me.

"Do yah have any beer in da house? Ya thick little sod, any beer, " he said laughing.

"No. I haven't," I replied.

"A useless little fucker you are, aren't you then?" he said laughing.

"No, I'm not," I replied, "you are."

"What if I box ya lugs for ya then?" he said now unable to stop laughing.

"If you touch me Don will batter you?" I threatened.

"Oh, will he now boy," The other one piped up.

"I will give him a thumping and den clout you, how's that for ya?"

At this point, I decided to go in the house and spy on them so they couldn't threaten me.

They threw the tarmac down, and one of the appeared with a bucket of red liquid and began pouring it all over the tarmac and then brushing it in with an old yard brush. I couldn't believe it looked like they had laid red carpet. Then out of nowhere next door's, ginger, tom cat appeared and began rolling about on the red tarmac and until it was the same colour. One of the Irishmen picked up the brush and belted the cat with it, it scurried off howling. The men finished and knocked on the door.

"What time's ya dad back?" he asked me.

"He's not my dad, and I don't know" I answered.

"So you'se a little bastard then is you," he laughed again.

"Tell him I will call back later then," he said walking off to the van, right through the red dye.

Don arrived back, and I saw his face when he pulled in and spotted the mess on the front.

"WHAT THE FUCK IS THAT?" he shouted.

I told him they were coming back for their money and the car. I didn't tell him about the abuse they had given me in case he went mad and started fighting them. There was three of them and only Don there wasn't much I could do.

"Are they just?" he laughed.

About an hour later I heard their van pull up and a knock on the door. Don went over and told me to stay inside. I heard voices then shouting, so, ignoring Don, I went to have a look. One of the Irishmen was in the hedge looking dazed, and Don had the other by the collar and part of the other man's coat still in his hand. He threw the man he had hold of across the drive and thumped the other one in the side of the head. He pasted them all one after the other and was kicking them up the arse with such force I thought he must have damaged their rectums. Eventually, they realised this was a man they wouldn't beat and began backing away, but still shouting threats.

"Come back here, and I will put you all through that van window and bring anyone else, and I will have ********** deal with you," he said, naming a gangster.

The Irishmen got in their van and roared off never to return.

Don took it all in his stride and sat down and had a cup of tea like nothing had happened.

He had no occupation that you could write down such as bricklayer or office worker, he was a businessman, and I assumed it was because he was, like busy all the time. He would come in and out at all hours, and the phone never stopped ringing. It was Tony the shop, or George the cars, or Mike the meat. I didn't know who all these people were, but I found it exciting.

Don would open the boot of his car and say, "Take one."

It would be a new leather jacket or the latest digital watch or something. We would be driving around London and cars would stop us and money would exchange hands. They would talk about how did that one go, up in the Elephant and Castle, the other night, and such. Sometimes they would nod towards me before talking, and Don would say he's okay go ahead. There was money there, but Don was putting a lot into the renovation of the house.

As we neared the end, I began to feel isolated and needed friendship from people my own age, so I decided to get a full-time job. I was seriously thinking about the Army, but decided I was a little too young, so, I thought I would leave it a year or so, besides I was a little scared of making the decision. The careers office in London sent me on a wild goose chase looking for a job. When they had asked me what I was interested in I had said I am not sure maybe a trainee chef or something, it was an off the cuff remark because I didn't know and they took it literally that I was mad about cooking. I could boil water, but it was too late. They sent me to Barclays Bank Headquarters in central London where they had catering positions.

I arrived on time with smart clothes on and was led into a room where a man and a woman sat. They both looked immaculate in suits.

"Sit down," they offered. "Would you like tea or coffee or perhaps water?"

"WATER!" I thought I had never been offered water before.

"No. I'm ok," I answered.

"Right okay, Edward," said the woman looking through her papers.

"Could I have a copy of your CV please?"

I looked at her bewildered, "CV?"

"Curriculum Vitae," she said.

"Oh, yes," I said remembering the strange word the careers office had used for my application form.

I handed it over and immediately saw her eyebrows go up. She's impressed I thought. She whispered something to the man and handed him my CV he actually stifled a giggle and passed the CV back to the woman.

She looked at me now in a pitying way and said, "Have you come for the position of Sous Chef?"

Now I was completely baffled, was she on about a Chef called Sue? What was she on about?

"What?" I replied.

"Have you come about the position of Sous Chef she repeated?"

"What's a Sous Chef?" I asked.

It was all too much for the man, he burst out laughing and left the room unable to hide his amusement.

"Thanks," she said to his back as he left.

I could hear him pissing himself laughing outside. The woman herself was sniggering but trying to regain her composure.

"Look you're not really suitable for this position," she managed, "I am sorry," she added and stood up ushering me to the door.

As I walked out past the various desks, people looked over laughing. What did I do I thought? I don't know what a bloody sous chef is.

As a parting shot, she said, "Go and see if you can find some manual work."

Eventually, I found myself a job in a factory packing cat litter in boxes. It was not the career I had in my mind, but I reasoned it would do for now and give me some money. The factory was just over the road from the apartment we had moved from in Collier Row, so it meant getting a train to Romford and then getting a bus.

My first day was awkward it was a workforce of middle aged women. Who treated me as though I was ten years old again.

"Do you need a wee?" they would ask and offer me sweets and stuff.

I had never been in the company of such people for any period of time, and I was at a loss to keep up with their gossiping on every subject under the sun. When one of them went to the toilet, the others would talk behind her back until the next one went and it was her turn. I watched fascinated as they filled bags with cat litter from a big peddle operated pump and then run the full bag through an industrial sewing machine to seal it without even looking and all this luminous still gossiping. Sometimes they would turn to me and start interrogating me as to why a Scouse urchin had fallen into this Essex factory. I was reluctant to get into a conversation about my past, and they sensed this and exploited it and teased me. The work itself was mind numbingly boring, but it was a chance to meet new people and get out the house and give me some money. There were about two or three people my own age one lad who dressed like Elvis with the brothel creeper shoes and leathers, he finished it with a big oily quiff and curled his lip like Elvis while talking.

I cracked up laughing every time, and he would say, "'Ere what you laughin' at you Scouse bastard?" in his cockney accent.

It wasn't long before I made friends with them all and I would go out and meet them, telling Don I was going to the cinema. London was ahead a little bit, and there were loads in the gang who were punks and such so we would hang about Romford all having a laugh but not on the scale as I did back home. It was just burgers and the odd bit of booze. One girl, I became friendly with, told me she got the same bus from Romford to Collier Row, and she had seen me a few times. She had a boyfriend but said she was going to finish with him. I sensed an opportunity, and it cheered me up.

"I will say hello next time," she said, "if my boyfriend is not with me."

A few weeks later I was on the way to work, and I would usually toss my sandwiches over the railway station wall because my sister put cheese on them every day without exception, I liked cheese, but after a month or two I could not eat any more cheese. However, this day I decided to keep them as I was feeling hungry. I caught the train to Romford and boarded the bus to Collier Row. My heart missed a beat when I spotted the girl I had become friendly with. However, her ugly boyfriend was sat next to her, but we exchanged a weak smile without him noticing. I was trying to play it cool and look grown up like the big man going to work. The bus was a typical London red with an open back platform. As my stop approached, I made my way to the back walking as cool as I could, and then I leaned against the pole as it approached still trying to look the man. The bus slowed as it reached the corner just before my stop and there was a small gap in the railings which I could go through, and it would save me walking back from the stop which was a bit further on. I glanced back to see if she was looking, she was, and she was smiling.

"She is in love with me," I thought, "why wouldn't she be, I was successful good looking and grown up? What wasn't to like? It was a no brainer, her ugly boyfriend or a Scouse stud?"

The gap in the railing approached, and I stepped off the still moving bus giving my babe a final glance back as I did. Her eyes were wide open, and her mouth was hanging and what the fuck??

I just remember going upside down, flying over the railings, seeing slices of bread fly into the air, hearing people scream, gasp and then the pain as I slid to a halt. The bus was gone, and people came running over.

"Oh, are you, all right?" they said helping me up.

"You're a silly little boy, aren't you?" one woman said, "Jumping off a moving bus like that."

"Oh, look he's dropped his lunch," someone said.

"I'm okay," I said staggering off with embarrassment.

I had scuffed my knees and elbows, but I felt consumed with shame. I never caught the same bus again and decided to leave the job a week or so later. I also never met up with the gang again. I couldn't have faced the girl. I started helping Don again, but the now self-imposed isolation from mixing with people my own age was becoming difficult. Don was good company and a good man, but he wasn't like my friends back home.

I was stuck between a rock and a hard place. I missed my mates back home, but I didn't want to go back home to the house as I knew it still lacked the essentials of comfort, I had now become used to. Don't get me wrong things were better in a sense I now had the freedom to come and go and fully support myself without hindrance, but my mother was still drinking, and I wasn't too sure if I could cope with all that again. I stayed on for a while longer and then made the decision to return home. I thought if it is no good I can just leave again.

So, I boarded the train and returned home. I was shocked at my mother's appearance. She certainly looked more frail and ill since I had left but she was still drinking! It was good to see all my mates again, and they mostly had jobs themselves except one or two who hadn't really done anything. The one thing I did notice is that I had grown a lot and it showed. I was a lot taller and no longer the short arse in the gang.

I was however now however desperately in need of a job to support myself, and I began a frantic search. It wasn't long before I got a break and was offered a job in the local Cadbury's factory where my dad worked, and I had stolen chocolate fingers from many times in the past. I was to be what they called a serviceman, which meant I would get the biscuits from a cold storage room, by hand pulled trolley, and take them to the end of a production belt, where numerous women would feed them through a machine that covered them in chocolate. It sounded easy, but it was in fact quite hard because they went through a phenomenal amount of biscuits and the store was some distance away. The factory was understandably hot, and it was hard work keeping up at first. The biscuits were in metal trays stacked on top of each other up to about seven-foot-high, so it was necessary to throw a strap around the load to stop it toppling over.

One day, I was under pressure as the belt was moving fast and so the women were demanding I was faster. I went into the store room where the biscuits were. It was used by many people so it was busy sometimes and there would be half loads people had taken back at the end of the shift. Even though you were supposed to take half loads first no one did because it was a full journey just for half the stock and meant coming back twice. Everyone would move a half load to get at a full load. I was doing exactly that when the full load toppled over spilling biscuits all over the floor. I was in a dilemma should I stay and of them up and then risk a major bollocking because the belt would run out or just leave them and deny it as others had done and get my load? I grabbed another load and made of very quickly. Later on, when

I returned for another load, the storeman was in the process of cleaning my mess up. I felt guilty as he scooped up all the broken biscuits moaning as he did so.

I began to get the hang of it and find short cuts, and the job became easier but also very tedious. As young boys and girls working together, we would all get up to mischief and no good, playing around on the trolleys and such. One lad suggested to me that if he got on the trolley, he could scoot down a huge ramp and if I opened the electronic door at the right moment and raised it a few feet he would be able to ride underneath it. He pulled his trolley up the huge ramp which had a bend in it so he would only see the door at the last minute.

I heard him shout from around the bend, "Ready?"

"Yes!" I hollered back, "Go!"

"Are you sure?" he shouted back nervously.

"Yes. GO!" I replied.

I heard a low rumble as he approached, it got louder and louder, and then he appeared around the bend like an Olympic bobsleigh, the wind flapping at his hair. He had approached the point of no return and saw that I hadn't raised the door.

With a look of absolute horror on his face, he began shouting, "DOOR! DOOR! OPEN THE FUCKING DOOR! PLEASE! PLEA...!"

He hit the corrugated tin door with such force it detached, and the bang must have sounded throughout the factory. He slid down it and melted on to the floor moaning. I realised I might have gone too far and ran over to him pretending that the door wouldn't open. As he began to recover, he also began getting angry.

"You're dead when I get up," he was muttering, "you done that on purpose."

"No, I didn't," I pleaded.

He was having none of it, so I made good my escape. And besides people were beginning to arrive to see what the noise was about.

As the money was really good in Cadbury's on a Friday, we would all be buzzing at the prospect of a night out to the local nightclubs in New Brighton. As I could now get in, by showing my birth certificate, I was also buzzing, and as 5 pm arrived, I was taking my trolley up to the refrigerated storage room. For some reason that escapes me, I was working in the cake department where they made gateaux. I came out of the lift but for some reason, the lights were out, and it was pitch black. I reached out and switched them on.

As they flickered to life, I just caught sight of someone approaching me fast, and then there was a thud, and everything went black. I pulled whatever was on my face off and then there was another thud. I realised I was under attack from pineapple gateaux. Two of the idiots I was working with had hidden in the storeroom and ambushed me. I was covered in cream and cake, then a cake fight started. It was like a Buster Keaton movie cakes flying all over. I got hit in the face again by a pineapple gateau that only my nose was sticking out the other side. The fun over we began to survey the mess and realised if caught we would be sacked for sure. Once again it was time to scarper. It was criminal really and juvenile at best. I am certain had we sat down and thought about it we wouldn't have done it.

Life at home was still dominated by my mother's drinking in that she was consumed by it, and so were we. For the very first time though she required a spell in hospital as the alcohol took its toll. She had gone to see my brother, Pete, and his wife, Edie, at their home in London, when she took ill and was admitted to the King George Hospital. After a week or so she was transported to our local hospital by ambulance. It was all a bit too much for me, and I closed my mind to what was really going on because I didn't like the reality of it all.

As anyone knows who has a relative or friend with alcohol problems things seem to go on for a long time and then quickly begin to unravel and this is what was happening. I never once asked my family what was going on or what their opinion or prognosis was but I sensed things were getting beyond serious. Now that I was old enough to look after myself and have total independence I also began to realise the severity of alcohol addiction.

In my mother's case, she was educated and could have had a million options in another time or place. If she was around now, it would be more than likely that she would have gone to university or at the very least been in a good job. But because of circumstances and timing she ended up raising far too many children and in that way, she sacrificed her own life for ours and she got little in return. Yes, she was loved, but I think that love was diluted by the circumstances of alcohol in that she might have not realised and on my part, there was the character created by the bottle that I loathed. It was still her, still looked like her, but as though she was taken over by someone else and I didn't like it, but then when she was sober, it was the nice mum again. That was the saddest part, the real person, who she was, missed out on so much because of alcohol. I sometimes wonder if she never had drunk how different life would have turned out not just for us but for her. She should have had the chance to watch us grow up, she should have been able to travel abroad and see the things she saw on television that fascinated her, like wildlife shows and such. She never got to taste champagne or smell the scent of the flowers in in hot countries or watch all her grandchildren grow up, meet my wife and my two beautiful children and grandchildren. I could go on and get bitter, but I won't be bitter or say it's not fair because life is not fair. But a decent human being went far too early because she tried to give too much, my mother.

Stewy Martindale had decided to take the plunge and join the army. As I was going stir crazy in Cadbury's, I felt as though it was a good option for me also but I was still unsure as to join or not. One day I was sure and the next I wasn't, so, I thought I would see what Stewy said when he got home on his first leave and then I could quiz him. A few weeks later he phoned to say he would be coming home the following weekend and we arranged to meet a local pub in Moreton Cross on the Friday.

On the night, another lad and I went to the pub to wait for him. We had about two beers each, and he still hadn't turned up. The pub was packed, as it was a Friday, and I wondered if he had looked in and not seen us.

"I tell you what," I said to the lad with me, "I will go and see if I can see him and have a look in the pub over the road you wait here and if he comes in I will see you in a minute."

"Okay," he agreed.

I made my way out of the pub, as people shuffled in and out. As I walked around a small bend from the pub, I noticed a few lads standing by the outside of the bank in front of me. I didn't take any real notice though as they seemed preoccupied and were chatting to each other. I passed them looking for Stewy when I felt a thud and sharp pain in my back. I realised I had been hit with a pellet gun. I turned around to confront the lad who had clearly shot me. He looked at me, smirking, as I moved closer. I made a huge mistake though I turned my back on the others with him and that was the last I remember. From what I have been told I was hit from behind as cowards do. I spent a few days in the hospital with a very sore head and a swollen face. The incident shook me as I was young, but it was also a very good lesson in life.

Strangely enough, I never saw any of those lads again, but the father of the one who hit me was a local drunk, who was regularly carried from the pub in a complete drunken stupor. He had some vague notion he was the 'Daddy', but in reality, he was a beer swilling coward just like the son he knocked out, probably, again while he was drunk. He has since died which almost gives dying a bad name.

As a result of this attack I never really got to chat with Stewy, and he went back leaving me pondering but with lots of unanswered questions. The Army was beginning to look like my best option of doing something with myself, as I had no qualifications, but I knew I wanted to learn. I would at least get to see Germany, which was a whole lot further than anywhere else I had travelled. It would also give me the opportunity to grow up and gain some experience in life. I wasn't sure what experience but I had very little at this point. I was also getting into a rut of working all week and spending it going out at weekends which was becoming monotonous.

I plodded on at Cadbury's with a sense that my time there was coming to an end one way or another for my own sanity. With that in mind, I decided that it was time I learned to drive and got a car. So, I began lessons, and someone suggested buying a car, and in between lessons I could then also learn in my own time with someone qualified sitting next to me. I took a loan out for about £300, which in those days was a good amount of money. My sister, her boyfriend at the time, my mum and dad were the only ones at home at the time, all the others were working away. I looked at a number of cars but didn't see any I liked. So, I left the money in my bed side cabinet for when I did see something.

One day I finally found a car I liked, and I went to get my money from the cabinet only to find it had disappeared! I was confused at first thinking I might have mislaid it but finally, the realisation dawned on me, I was beside myself with hurt that someone would do that. I know with all my heart it wasn't my mum, who was by now very frail or my dad, who never stole anything in his life. Only two people knew of that money and where it was hidden my sister and her boyfriend. I searched the house again and again to no avail. I finally had to tell the lad I had changed my mind and didn't want the car, which was the complete opposite, as I really wanted it. I told my sister about the money when she came in, and she said she didn't know anything about it, but on cue, her boyfriend had disappeared off somewhere, almost answering who was the guilty party in doing so. He has since died and is the father of one of my nieces, so the matter is ended as far as I am concerned, but at the time I had to work extra shifts to pay the debt off and all for nothing.

I stopped my driving lessons and resumed just plodding on, working and going out. I was bored but the weekends did offer some relief from the monotony of Cadburys and the developing strain of my mother's failing health at home.

I went out, one Saturday, with a mate, and for some reason, we ended up bumping into my older brother, Boe, who was out. We had all been to a few pubs and were drunk and in high spirits. We went to a Chinese restaurant. It was snowing and very slippy under foot, but we arrived and were shown a table.

The place was a little tired and could have done with a clean, but in our drunken state, I guess we weren't too fussy. We ordered our food and yet more beer and were generally being a pain in the ass because we thought we were smart and funny. I knew I had just about enough money to cover my meal and drinks, but that was about it. I was half eating my meal and struggling to keep it on the fork when in an instance my brother and mate made for the door and disappeared leaving their empty plates and glasses behind. It took a second through my alcohol fudged brain to realise what they had done. There was no way I could cover their meals and drinks even if I had wanted to, which I didn't. I was up on my feet and following them. As I reached the door, I heard very loud and aggressive shouting from the Chinese waiter who was watching his profits go out the door.

Somewhere in his Cantonese dialect, I could hear the words, "Bastards."

As I came out the door, my feet went from under me as I hit the snow. I heard a thud, and then a whoosh as the same fate had fallen on the Chinese waiter only he slid past me and was now in front of me. I scrambled to my feet, as did he. He was skidding backwards and forwards trying to grab my coat, and I was bending over backwards so he couldn't get a purchase on my collar. People were walking past laughing at what must have looked like a Laurel and Hardy sketch. Finally, I got a foot hold and began running with the Chinese waiter behind me, and then he slipped landing on his arse with a thud. His threats faded as I made distance and finally got away. I was sweating and threw up with all the effort. So much for a free dinner.

As I walked, I caught sight of my brother and friend walking ahead without a care in the world laughing and joking with each other. As I caught them up, they both burst out laughing and so did I.

"Come on," my brother said, "we can walk over the bridges across the docks and get a taxi home."

I agreed I'd had enough drama for one night. As we crossed over the bridge on the docks, my brother spotted a small boat tied up. It was only small with a small cabin and old. It was a few yards out on its tether, and in his wisdom, my brother decided he would be able to make the leap from the dock on to the boat. I wasn't sure, and it was a freezing night so going into that water could kill, but again the alcohol subdued all common sense.

"It's easy," he boasted.

He took a few steps back ran and landed on the boat. I grabbed the tether and pulled him into the dock. He climbed off.

"Now your turn," he said looking at me.

"No, I've had too much to drink," I protested.

"Coward," he goaded, "scaredy cat."

"Scared? Fuck off, it's easy," I came back feeling annoyed.

He gave the boat a shove, so it drifted out to the full length of the tether.

"Go on," he said.

Like an idiot, I relented and said, "OK."

Wearing flared trousers and platform shoes, which were at the height of fashion at the time, I ran towards the boat and launched myself off the dock wall and landed perfectly on it.

"Ha Ha, easy," I shouted at my brother and mate who were both laughing.

Only they were laughing far too loud and much too long. I reached for the tether to pull myself back to the dock when I heard a splash. I looked up to see my brother had unleashed the rope and the boat was now drifting away from them with me on it. They stood on the dock wall laughing and waving.

"You better get me back here you fucking bastard!" I yelled at them.

"Or what?" my brother shouted back laughing.

"As soon as I get off here you're dead!" I screamed.

"Oh, I'm shaking in my boots," he mocked.

"I'm telling me, dad," I said as a last resort.

"Oh dear, what he going to do come around and tell my wife to put me on the naughty step."

They walked off and left me. It was pitch black, cold and I was panicking. I did consider jumping off and swimming to the side, but it wasn't really an option. I looked around the boat for a paddle or something I could use to at least try and get to the dock wall, but there was nothing at all. I tried lying flat and paddling with my hand, but it wouldn't reach. Then I had a brainwave. I took my shoe off and put my leg over the side and tried to paddle using my foot but it was useless, my foot was frozen in a moment and painful. I sat there wondering what to do. I could see lights on in buildings on the docks, but I was scared to shout out. I almost felt like crying. I was racking my brains what to do, but it was pointless. I then wondered if I would just drift back in or could I drift out the dock and into the River Mersey or even out to sea. I was also getting cold. My jacket was damp where I had fallen in the snow earlier. There was a bit of tarpaulin on the back so I wrapped it around me and decided I couldn't do anything, I really was up the creek without a paddle this time.

I must have fallen asleep because I woke with a start to a voice.

"What are you doing, have you lost power?

I looked up to see a policeman looking down at me from the dock wall.

"What are you doing?" he asked again but in a much sterner voice.

"Officer help," I pleaded, "this isn't my boat some lads made me jump on it, or they said they were going to throw me in the water."

A small boat also came alongside, and another policeman jumped on board. I told him the story, and he began checking about the boat. Seeing that the lock to the cabin was untouched, my story became believable. I started crying not because of the fictitious thugs, though that would have been a fair description of my brother and mate but because I was relieved to be saved.

"It's okay," they said helping me off the boat.

I had to go through the whole story and made up a description of these lads.

"We need to catch these two idiots," the policemen said, "you could have gone into that icy water, and it would have been your body we were pulling out."

"Yes," I agreed.

I had to give the officers my details and a brief statement of what happened. It was getting light, and I knew that my brother and mate would be tucked up in bed, bastards!

"Okay, we are done here," the officer said, "would you like a lift home after your ordeal."

"Yes, please officer," I replied.

He kindly took me home.

Later that day I went to see my brother in a foul mood, but he was just laughing and taking the piss. I did consider all kinds of ways of getting revenge, but I began to see the funny side of it in the end. Years later I did my Royal Marines swimming test in the same dock.

My penchant for being chased by Chinese food workers didn't seem to diminish much. A few years later, having consumed a fair amount of alcohol on a wild night out, with Mick Price, we succumbed to hunger but had spent all our money and didn't have enough for a packet of crisps between us. So, we decided in our drunken wisdom that the answer was to order some food from a Chinese chippy in Moreton Cross and run away with the food without paying. It seemed like the perfect plan, and nothing could really go wrong!

At the time, we were in an old car Mick was driving so we tossed probably the only money had a one pence piece to see who would do the hit and who would be the getaway driver. Mick lost the toss and would go and get the food, and I would be the getaway driver.

"Okay, what you want," he said, sitting with a pencil and writing the order on a small piece of plaster board he had found in the car.

"Ok," I said, "I will have sweet and sour pork, half chips, half rice, prawn crackers and get me a spare portion of chips, and..."

"Fuck off," Mick said, "that will do. I've got to run with all this lot."

"Okay," I relented, "just that then. What you having?" I asked him.

He sat pondering and then began scribbling his order down, which was that long he had to turn the plaster board over. I snatched off him.

"Fuck me. Look how much you've ordered for you, you greedy twat," I said.

"I'm the main runner," he said, "wait here with the car running."

He jumped out, and I sat with the engine ticking over. Minutes ticked by and it seemed like ages. I thought he had been gripped before he even got out the door when he came running out the chippy with all the meals stacked up so I high it was a wonder he could see where he was going. The Chinese lad was hot on his heels. Mick was running from side to side like a gazelle trying to outwit a cheetah. It was the funniest sight I had seen in my life. I could hear the Chinese lad shouting and swearing as they neared the car. Two meals fell off the stack as Mick cornered around the bonnet of the car and jumped in the passenger seat.

"Was that my dinner you just dropped?" I shouted as he sat panting.

"Fucking drive!" he screamed.

I went to pull off and STALLED. The Chinese lad yanked at my door as I gunned the engine back into life and we sped away. I just caught sight of his angry face as he disappeared from my window. We drove off and parked on the shore laughing.

"You fucking stalled, you dickhead," Mick laughed.

"Well you dropped two meals, you dickhead," I retaliated.

"What were the ones you dropped?" I asked.

"Just spare," he said laughing.

We sat and ate our spoils totally unconcerned that it was stolen food. It might have been youth or not thinking about it but it was not right I know that now but it was all part of life's rich tapestry to us and reality was something to worry about when we got older.

Moreton Shore and lighthouse, the place we harassed courting couples.

My mother fell off the precipice of life and became very ill, and even to me it was now obvious she was dying, and that really is when the reality hit me. I -had a mixture of sorrow and panic. My mind was in a state of turmoil and confusion. It was now August 1979, and two of my sisters had returned home to take care of my mother who was unable to do the simplest tasks such was her poor condition.

One day she had been taken down to the garden and laid back in a chair with a quilt wrapped around her. I was a beautiful hot sunny day with birdsong and bees, and the distant sound of children playing and the scent of flowers and grass floated on the warm breeze. Birds swooped going about their innocent lives without a care in the world. Planes flew overhead with people going to foreign destinations, places my mother would never see or experience, for someone so passionate about wildlife it was an injustice at best.

I was sat on a chair in the garden when I glanced across and saw my mother sitting watching it all, soaking up every sight and every sound. She was experiencing the last days of her life on earth, and I wonder what she thought. She would never see the snow again, she would never see another winter's night. Hear the birds sing or listen to the wind blow. Watch the clouds dance across the sky or feel the rain on her face.

I was 18 years old, and I didn't really want all this I wanted it to be someone else who had this burden on their shoulders but me. I avoided going into the bedroom where my mother was because I felt scared, awkward and if I am truly honest a little angry she had done this by drinking too much. It was only years later that the realisation of what she coped with and the grip alcohol has that I fully understood that she was a victim and very helpless to her fate.

My father carried on going to work, but I don't really know what he felt at this time or how he coped, but it must have been so hard on him.

I got up at five am, as I was on the early shift at my mundane job in Cadbury's.

I was working away when one of the bosses approached me and said, "You're wanted over the surgery son."

"What for?" I asked.

"I don't know," he replied.

He knew, and so did I but I kidded myself it could be something entirely innocent.

I walked into the surgery to see my dad sitting in a chair sobbing. He looked up at me when I walked in.

"Your mother's died son," he said.

I broke down crying and walked back over to the factory. I got changed and headed home with my dad. When we arrived back at the house, I walked into the hall to see a blue coloured steel coffin. My sisters were there grim faced and with the strain of what we had all been through etched on their faces. I went up to my room and sat on my bed, and my thoughts were fragmented at best. I was confused as to what would happen now. Who does what, what do we say? I mean this was my first real encounter with death. It had come into my life and introduced itself regardless of how young I was or if I was ready or not.

People began arriving at the house, and I could hear crying downstairs. I felt awkward and as though I wanted to hide away from it all. I wished I could have got in bed and hidden under the blanket.

Over the next few days, we all walked around lost. My mother had gone but so had the familiarity of her being sick and dependent and her ringing the little bell she had to attract attention. There was no one there now who need help. There was no purpose to keeping quiet if she was sleeping or the routine to looking after someone sick. She was no longer dependent or indeed sick. She didn't need help or anything from us anymore. It was a brutal conclusion to a life lived no less. It was us, we mere, weak human beings who needed help for grief and pain. We were now the weak ones. My mother was no longer in pain or hungry, thirsty or tired but we were.

Were all these things the payoff for the nice things like watching the sun set or the birds fly. Did everything have its price in this world? For enjoying a nice meal did you have to have indigestion? For enjoying a few glasses of fine wine, did it mean you paid with a hangover? I began to look at life more deeply because of my mother's death. I did come to the realisation that we are all going to die sooner or later, and as silly as that maybe I didn't really consider my own fate until then. The reality of life had taken its first of many bites from my arse and metaphorically speaking I still have every scar.

The house I had grown up in, the pokey little three-bedroom council allocated hovel with mould on the walls in my room, and the frozen windows in winter had become even bleaker in my mind. I had frankly never liked it because it was a place of utter misery and bad memories. I knew my days of living there were nearing the end and I was happy at that thought.

The day of my mother's funeral arrived, and we gathered outside Bleak House as the hearse came into the road carrying her coffin. I climbed into the funeral car along with my sisters, and it made its way slowly down our road. The same way my mother had trudged up and down in all weathers carrying shopping and babies and coal and all manner of things to keep the house going. She had made endless trips up and down this road looking for money to feed us or go to the two or three jobs she had to make ends meet.

And now she was leaving forever killed by an addiction that subtlety offered her relief during the darkest and most desperate of times in her quest to look after her expanding and dependent brood of children. And now that liquid medicine was, after all, shown for what it really was, poison, and it had taken its payment in full. We held my mother's funeral on a warm hot, glorious day and patted each other on the backs and I listened to old stories of my mother lost in time, and I laughed knowing her character. The crowd eventually broke up, and we dispersed to our own lives. A chapter of my life had ended.

I returned to work at Cadbury's but I was changed, I was less shy and more determined than ever that this wasn't going to even be my present let alone my future. I carried on for a while and then I made the move and joined the army. I felt at this point that I really had run out of options and it was now or never. So, I left Cadburys and enlisted into the Royal Artillery, and that part of my life was also over.

I have no regrets about my childhood because it was what it was, there is no changing it. Yes, it could have been better, I could have lived a more comfortable life, had a nice home and all the things the other kids got, like new bikes, even decent clothing and a school uniform would have made all the difference, but it wasn't to be. The bullies were just children, and they saw something different, and I understand that now. My own misgivings and some of the stealing and such were just as bad. I doubt however had I have lived in a different environment that I would have been such a little tearaway.

As a child, I adapted to what was going on around me, and that is not an excuse. Children are by nature very perceptive. I do regret however not getting the education I think all children are entitled to. Education is everything, and it is one of the key factors to success. I also believe it gives a person confidence and discipline. On many occasions in my life, I have known someone to be wrong about something or a subject, and I didn't have the confidence to speak up and correct them. I had some good teachers in school who tried their best but knew my situation was rather hopeless, but there were one or two who were a disgrace to the profession and their only input into my already miserable life was to try and make it more so. I really am at a loss as to why the authorities at the time allowed us to go unschooled without making any real efforts to find out why. The real tragedy, however, is the lost years that I could have been learning and getting qualifications that would have carried me forward.

That said how do you measure success? Is it at the final count what you own or how much money you have, the size of your house or car? Well I own my own home, I have a brand new expensive car, and I have been on expensive holidays, but I measure my success like this. I have two children Kristy and Nathan. I have a grandson, Henry, from Kristy and a granddaughter on the way. Kristy is married to a wonderful and compassionate man, my son in law, Adam. Nathan is married to a beautiful and caring girl Jenny. I am lucky enough to have the most beautiful and caring wife any man could wish for Tricia who I love with all my heart forever. I measure that love and those people as success over and above everything. Nothing else matters.

The author in Berrylands Road, going to join The Army, with all I owned in one tiny bag

The author after finishing basic training in the Army, Woolwich, London

My beautiful wife, Tricia, and I

Author, Moreton Shore, aged 55

Author's son, Nathan, with wife, Jenny

With my grandson, Henry

Author's daughter, Kristy, with husband, Adam, grandson, Henry and granddaughter, Ophelia

I went on to serve nearly 10 years in the British Army specialising in anti-aircraft missile systems. I fought in the Falklands War and served in Northern Ireland where I injured my knees bringing my career to an end. I have chronicled my military career in my book "Not for Queen and Country" which is also available on Amazon Books.

On leaving the Army, I had numerous bilateral knee operations which were by and large unsuccessful and having been in peak physical condition while in the army I really was up against it and not used to being infirm. During these times, my wife Tricia had to not only cope with raising our two children but try and visit me in hospital.

It wasn't just the pain I suffered in my knees, I had suffered terrible nightmares since serving in the Falklands War. I would wake up in the morning totally exhausted. I also felt depressed and hopeless. I put it down to my ongoing knee problems, and I tried to ignore it, and finally, I started to drink alcohol with my mates down the pub. All familiar territory but the alcohol offered me a window of calm. It was that first couple of drinks that slew my anxiety and made me feel normal, happy carefree. I should have known the pitfalls, but I either didn't see them or chose to ignore them. After that few drinks had turned into several, I would feel even more depressed and the next day was even worse.

The people I was drinking with were not real friends anyway apart from Mick Price. It was he who cared and wanted to know what I had been through. I was under no illusions about the rest of them they were fair weather friends, including a lad I had attended school with, who was now more Mick's mate than mine and he who hated the military talk.

My drinking was taking off at a pace and affecting my judgement and ability to make decisions; I woke up one day with more than a hangover. I felt on the edge of a nervous breakdown, and I realised it was time to really look at what was bothering me and once and for all address it. I also knew I would never get drunk again. There was no epiphany it was a decision, and I knew I was never going to sit getting drunk ever again. Sure, I would drink, but I would always keep it to a point where I was in control and not the alcohol.

I analysed my life at that moment, and even though my childhood had been hard, I knew my time in the Falklands War and Northern Ireland had affected me. At that point, in 1990, it wasn't trendy to admit you had a mental health problem and doing so in the Army would have ended anyone's career. Thankfully in that regard, I was a civilian, but I was still unsure of what to do. I would go through so many emotions. Should I tell my Doctor, or contact the army? I quickly dismissed approaching the Army as a non-option and remarkably I didn't have much idea about Combat Stress. I thought it was just an organisation that looked after old men who had been in World War 2. I decided to go and see my doctor. I was so nervous when I walked in I fluffed my rehearsed speech and beads of sweat were rolling off my face.

"I don't feel, in my head!" I blurted out.

"I have been waiting for you to come in about this," he replied.

I was confused, how did he know? He put his pen down and looked at me.

"I have known you were struggling for some time," he said.

"However, I don't think you would have agreed had I told you at the time so I waited for you to come to me."

The tears came rolling down my cheeks.

"Right, you're right," I nodded.

"I know I am," he replied but not in a smug way.

"So now we can begin treating you," he said.

I felt a weight lift off my shoulders, I had made the first move, and no one had told me to pull myself together or laughed. I was suffering from Post-Traumatic Stress Disorder. My doctor assured me that I wasn't going mad or weak or an embarrassment. I began taking medication and for the first time in my life gaining a real understanding of what this condition was.

My friend, Mack, who I served with in the Falklands, with was crushed by it, but I was still unsure as to what was wrong with me until now. I came to understand that I was, in old parlance, suffering from 'Battle Shock'. It felt as though I was letting the side down. Was I a weak link in the chain? All my insecurities from my childhood began to rise. Was I that weak that I couldn't cope with war or conflict?

I was a broken man because I had watched people die and been under threat of life or was it that I was just weak at everything? As I learned more, I began to accept that I wasn't weak or cowardly but a man with feelings and emotions and it is not normal to witnesses such horrors, and the mind has its way of dealing with these images and threats. In fact, it is not a disorder at all, it is to cope with it all. 'Battle shock' has been around since man himself.

I recall with sadness someone finding out I was being treated for PTSD and saying, "I would keep that to yourself or you will be the subject of ridicule."

At the time, I nodded in agreement because I knew no better. However, knowing what I know now I would tell that same person to go and tell those who would mock me and had never been in a war to go and get lost. I know Mack received many e mails calling him a coward for speaking up about the subject and the irony is that those same people are now more than happy to promote PTSD because it is now socially acceptable. How I despise those sycophants.

My nightmares continue but they are now part of my life. When I go to sleep each night, I know where I am going because it's common ground. I really hope that the soldiers who return from battle in future wars are well looked after regarding both their physical and mental health and that we continue to evolve better methods of treatment for those we ask to make the ultimate sacrifice. Make no mistake asking someone to commit to war is asking them to put their life on the line for a cause that they might not believe in but they have taken the oath and for a small wage they honour it. The least society can do is keep their promise to look after those who return damaged in battle.

In 1996 my father's health began to fail, he was 78 years old and apart from some age-related illness he was up to this point in relatively good health. He was still walking to the shops a couple of miles away to get his paper and going to bed with a whiskey to listen to his radio. The years had mellowed him for sure, he had become less regimented. He was hit by a minor stroke that took it out of him but left no real residual effects.

However, in the June of 1996, I got a phone call to say he was still in bed rather late in the day, which wasn't like him at all and that it appeared he had, had a stroke. Why the fact he was still in bed so late as an early riser all his life had not been picked up by a family member remains a mystery to me even to this day. I know that if my father had not risen as normal, it would have aroused my suspicions! I drove to the old family home in time to see my father being put into the back of an ambulance.

I got in the back where he lay on the stretcher and said, "Dad, it's Eddy, you are going to be alright."

I didn't really know if he would be alright and if he, was convinced but it was all I could think of.

It was as we suspected another stroke but this time it was more critical. My father was admitted to the stroke ward and over the next few days we learned he would not recover this time and his life was near the end. In the first few days, he was sat up and fully conscious. He began to slip into a coma, and his life started to ebb away as his organs began to shut down. I looked at him in the hospital bed and thought of all he must have seen in the war while serving in the Navy and crossing the submarine infested waters of the Atlantic. The massive brood of children he had brought in to the world who had now produced many grandchildren. A well-aimed German torpedo would have changed all that!

I left the hospital to go and shower after being there for a long time and on my arrival home was greeted with the news that my father had died just after I had left. I was devastated at the loss but this time older, wiser and more prepared than when my mother had died. I served in the Falklands and Northern Ireland, so the concept of death wasn't new anymore.

We said farewell to my dad on a hot sunny afternoon just like my mother. So that was it I had no parents now, and it did feel strange and even more so when I considered how many people I knew who still had their mum and dad. The only consolation was that my dad was now reunited with my mother and if that was so, I hope they really are now together for eternity. The old family home is now in the hands of another family member, but I do not and never will revisit it.

I had never once in my life despite the hardships and tragedy's I had faced thought of myself as having a raw deal in life when I knew some people had what can only be considered a smooth ride. I had known hunger and suffered bullying from a young age. I had lived through very desperate and very dark times from the start. I would have to say that life for me from childhood was mostly depressing with the odd moment of joy or distractions from real life while I was getting up to no good. But I reasoned as young as I was that this was meant to be how life was. It was never supposed to be nice and wonderful, it was a journey I would have to endure and then it would be over some day. All the nice things in life they were never meant for me and I accepted it as just what it was life. Had I have died in the Falklands War, at 21, that would have been that, but I survived and went on to learn that the good things in life and the happiness they belong to everybody, not just the privileged few.

The Falklands war changed me in that I really began to care much less for officialdom and authority. Who makes all the rules, who decides what is acceptable and what is not. Who has the right to tell me how to live my life and what I should think? No one is the real answer. Life is hard enough just by what fate has in store without anything else, and I soon learned that fate hadn't finished with me by a long way. You can sometimes fool yourself into believing that if you really have had more than your fair share of crap that fate will be kind and reasonable. Fate is fate it is not a living thing that makes decisions it's whatever comes your way good or bad or in some cases bad and then more bad.

Life for me had calmed down, and Tricia and I had bought a house which we were busy renovating, and I had just had my book, 'Not for Queen and Country', published so for once in a long while my life had become a bit easier and I was finally becoming content. I had also been out to New York on a fundraising trip with a friend and a group of firefighters from the Wirral. It was in aid of the 9/11 twin towers terrorist attack. I visited the remains of the buildings which was an experience I will never forget. So many lost lives and for what, some warped ideology that has no place in a modern world.

I recall this day with clarity. Tricia and I had driven to the supermarket, and I had asked if I could wait in the car as I didn't feel like facing the hassle. She agreed, and I waited outside on a warm August evening sitting listening to music in the car. I must have fallen asleep as Tricia woke me opening the boot of the car. I wondered where I was for a moment which is always the same for me waking up. We drove home and had dinner and settled down to watch some television. I eventually decided to go up to bed feeling tired. It was long before Tricia came up and I fell into a deep sleep.

I awoke with a start to the shrill sound of the house phone going. Tricia answered it, it was just after midnight, and I sensed something must be wrong because of the time. I caught snippets of what Tricia was saying down the phone and her expression which above all concerned me. My daughter, Kristy, and son, Nathan, were in bed, so I knew all was ok as far as they were concerned. Tricia put the phone down and informed me my older sister Ally had fallen on the stairs and suffered a head injury and she was now being treated in the local hospital Arrowe Park.

"What are her injuries?" I pressed Tricia.

"I don't know?" she answered, "But they said to go up now."

I was very concerned but certainly not panicking. We dressed quickly and drove to the hospital a couple of miles away. On arriving, I found one of my sisters who had been staying at Ally's that night. She had clearly been drinking which was par for the course with this particular sister. She was older than me, and if I am truly honest, I had never really liked her, and the less I saw of her, the better. She was being comforted by some older guy I had never met, but the fact he was up at the hospital made me realise she must have rung him first. That was the type of thing she would do so I wasn't surprised.

My sister Ally's son, one who was in his early teens, was there, so we had to be careful what we said and asked. Tricia and I approached my sister reluctantly on my part to try and find out how badly hurt Ally was and what had happened. I knew it was going to be hard work as she was clearly drunk but that said it would have been hard work if she was sober.

As expected we were told some half-baked story with much slurring and came away none the wiser as she carried on her drunken dramatics. From what we could make out from sister Ally had banged her head after falling on the stairs and was having a scan, and that was all the detail she gave us. I admit I was a little confused, but Tricia and I said we would go home and come and see Ally at home or if they kept her in we would return to the hospital tomorrow and see her. We drove home and went to bed. However, I couldn't sleep whether it was having to deal with the drunken sister who I dislike or the fact I felt something wasn't right I don't know, but I got up and went downstairs and put the TV on, I wasn't watching it I was far too distracted. The phone rang, it was my sister, Lin.

"Eddy," she said, "our Ally is on a life support machine, and she has an hour to live!"

"Wha...What," I said unable to process what she had just said. "Who told you that?" I asked her.

"The hospital has just said," she replied, "it's true. Can you get hold of Mary and Sue?" she asked, adding, "There's no reply from either of them, we have phoned and phoned their houses."

"Ok," I said my head spinning, "Tricia and I will come and get you then go to the hospital and see what is going on, then I will get them two."

We picked Lin up and drove to the hospital where the mood was very, very different to less than an hour earlier. This time the information was correct my sister Ally had suffered a catastrophic brain injury in the fall downstairs and was only being kept alive by the ventilator. I felt like just dropping to my knees I could hardly breathe with total grief. I knew I had to be strong though my nephews were there and this was their mum.

"Where are Mary and Sue?" I asked.

"We don't know," someone said, "we can't get hold of them."

Tricia and I made the decision to drive to Sue's house as we had an idea Mary and her husband John might be staying there. It was about a 10-mile drive from the hospital, so we set off a bit faster than normal. I was desperate that they see her alive and time was running out.

We arrived at the house to find it in total darkness as you would expect at two o'clock in the morning. I began banging on the door, but nothing stirred at all. In total frustration, I pounded on the door until I thought it was going to come off its hinges and finally a light went on in a bedroom, and a face appeared at the window.

"Open the fucking door!" I shouted up.

As the front of the house was totally dark, I could understand the reluctance to come down and open the door to such aggressive knocking. The face moved from the window only to be replaced by another face that looked equally alarmed at the sight outside. Eventually, the door was opened, and a face appeared in the small crack.

"It's Eddy and Tricia," I said pushing my way into the hallway.

My sister was standing looking as you would completely confused, not helped by the alcohol she had surely consumed.

"Where is Mary?" I asked, wondering where my other sister was. I wanted to get them all together, so I didn't have to keep repeating the devastating news.

"What going on?" Sue kept asking.

"Get Mary," I said.

She did, and eventually, Mary appeared on the landing, and it was apparent that she had also had a skin full. I knew then that getting to make them comprehend this tragedy wasn't going to be easy. I told them Ally had been in a serious accident and that we had to get to the hospital immediately. My sisters got dressed quickly and jumped into my car and set off for the hospital down the dark lanes. I was while we were driving that I dropped the bombshell that my sister Ally wasn't going to make it. I looked at my sisters in the back of my car in the rear-view mirror and in the light from the dashboard I could tell they hadn't understood what I had just told them. I told them again but a bit more brutally.

"She is going to die," I said firmly.

This time they looked like it might have sunk in, but Sue then said, "No, no we can sort it out and get her to a private hospital."

"No, we really can't, this is not about money or anything else it is too late for that now, and nothing is going to stop her dying," I said even feeling the emotion and sadness of those words on myself.

We arrived at the hospital, and more family had come. Everyone was ushered into a side room, where the doctor informed us that they were going to switch off the life support machine and to say our goodbyes now. We had been unable to get hold of my sister Jean and her husband John who lived in South Shields in time, but she had now been informed and was racing south. She would never make it in time sadly.

I had even tried our local police station to see if they could contact the police in South Shields and send a car to Jean's house as we knew she was in but couldn't hear the phone.

Merseyside police basically said to me "You sort it out!" The female officer told me to drive to South Shields myself!

All my family went into the resuscitation room to say their farewells to my sister Ally. I decided not to because I wanted to cherish the memory of her the last time I had seen her fit and well. On the morning of the 15th August 2002, the life support machine was switched off, and my sister Ally slipped away aged 42 years. She left two young sons who she adored and had just achieved her degree in Psychology from Chester University.

I felt my world collapse, and I was angry it seemed so unfair and yet another tragedy I had to deal with, but my real sorrow went out to her two sons, my nephews. I went home inconsolable and exhausted and fell into a very disturbed sleep, waking every 10 minutes or so, and realising that this nightmare was for my waking hours. Later, I went over to my sister Mary's house where some of the family were gathered apart from the sister who was with Ally, she wasn't there.

For the first time, I began asking questions of what happened and started getting some facts. Ally had been found at the bottom of the stairs unconscious and totally unresponsive with blood coming out of her ears and her little dog, Olly, yapping about her, concerned. Her younger son had found her even and given her the kiss of life, though he had only popped next door and my other sister was in bed and had apparently heard nothing!

When I was given these details, I was utterly astonished. The sister who had been with Ally and who we had spoken to at the hospital when Tricia and I had initially gone up there, never gave us any of this horrid detail leaving us to at first believe it was nothing more than a bang on the head. Had she have mentioned that fact Ally had blood coming from her ears I would have understood the seriousness of it straight away and began gathering the rest of the family. Instead, we returned home losing precious time. What was going through that sister's mind in neglecting to tell us these significant details I will never know and I never want to know.

That morning the police cordoned off her house as a crime scene which is the protocol for such events until foul play has been ruled out. Quite how they did this in the minimal time and very rudimentary investigation they did I don't know? I can only assume that they had already made their minds up before arriving or maybe there was a two for one offer on for breakfast at the local McDonalds. I've seen more attention paid by a policeman issuing a parking ticket.

We held my sister's funeral a week or so later, and it was well attended as she was very popular. A month later we had a remembrance service in Chester which was attended by lots of her university friends and lecturers. I guess it was a point in my life where my resolve to always accept life can be hard and that we must take the good and bad was tested. I felt like I had had enough of life's crap and that I had had my fair share of shit for a lifetime. If only.

I think more out of necessity to occupy my mind following my sister's death I began organising charity challenges. Firstly, in Australia, where I arranged for three friends to cycle down the notorious 'Birdsville Track', in the outback of Southern Australia, from Adelaide.

Another one of the team and I had to fly down to make initial contact and organise everything ahead of the main event. We flew from Manchester, via Singapore, and arrived in Adelaide completely worn out. We were greeted at the airport and taken to the fire station where we would be staying, or so that is what I had planned! After a quick shower, I said to the other lad I am going to get some sleep. Me too he said. I fell into a deep sleep only to be woken after what seemed like five minutes. It was the other lad.

"There's a firefighter here who has said we can go and stay in his house," he told me.

"But we are okay here, we have everything we need," I replied not understanding very well with the tiredness.

"Yes, but he has also offered to help us," he replied.

"Well okay," I relented getting out of bed.

I went and met this firefighter.

"G'Day," he said in an Australian twang.

"Hello," I replied.

He looked like he had just wrestled a crocodile. He shook my hand nearly breaking it.

"Okay," he went on, "load ya shit in the back of my truck and we can make a move."

The other lad whose bright idea this was, and I threw our bags into the back of Croc man's truck. I climbed in the back so I didn't have to engage in too much conversation on account of me not understanding a word Croc Man said and the fact he spat while he talked, I'd already had a shower.

He powered the truck out of the fire stations gates, and I fell asleep waking again with a bump as we hit a pothole. There was nothing but thick red dust and parched landscape. It looked like the surface of Mars.

"Ya back with us ya," was all I understood.

"Yes," I said with a mouth that felt like a kangaroo had dropped its joey in.

"We are just gonna call in at my golf club for a bite to eat and a drink and meet some of my friends," Croc Man informed me.

"Oh, fantastic," I said unconvincingly.

I wondered exactly where they would play golf having seen no grass, but I guess anything was possible here.

The truck pulled up at a small, tired looking building and we jumped out. My knees were aching from the flight and now having to sit in this truck. We followed Croc Man into the building and into a bar where there were people and families all drinking. Like anyone, when you go into somewhere like that, our mind is looking and assessing the environment and more importantly the people. Now don't get me wrong I've drunk in some rough places all over the world, but this place was 'Duel of the Banjos' from the film Deliverance. I thought it was only a matter of time before I would spread over the bar while they took turns. People had teeth missing and grinned at us through squinted eyes. The gene pool looked like it was out of sync for reasons only they knew.

Croc Man seeing me looking bewildered offered me a menu. It offered Schnitzel with fries, fries with egg or just fries!

"I will have the Schnitzel and fries with coke please," I said to the large greasy woman behind the counter.

"COKE! You bloody pom wuss," she sneered.

I laughed back weakly not wanting any misinterpretation. Cooky he pulled a discoloured and worn out plate from a rack beside her and shovelled a pile of over cooked and very greasy fries on to it and then plucked the Schnitzel from a boiling cauldron of black fat and slammed it on the plate, as she did so the stinking fat poured out of it. The smell of overcooked stale fat was overwhelming. However, Cooky wasn't done yet. She grabbed a bunch of leaves that looked like they had been treated with weed killer and put them on the plate along with a hefty amount of soil and shoved the plate towards me.

"Enjoy," she said coughing into her hand and wiping it on her dirty apron.

I sat down with my plate of Salmonella and began the task of pretending I was eating it.

"Not hungry?" Croc Man inquired, seeing me push the food about my plate.

"No," I lied, "just tired."

"Okay let's make a move then," he replied.

He must have seen the relief on my face. I couldn't believe we had got out without being sexually assaulted. Feel on the rest of the trip to Croc Man's house in case I needed to escape. We trundled further along the road for a while, and there wasn't much to see until I spotted a shack on stilts in the distance.

"Oh, please don't let that be his house," I said to myself, "please."

We carried on past, and I was so thankful until he made a sharp left down a dirt track and pointed to the shack on stilts.

"That's my house," he said with pride.

I sank back in my seat defeated. Don't get me wrong I have slept in some terrible places with the Army, but we had come to Australia, and we had left perfectly good clean accommodation for this.

We pulled up beside the shack, and I wasn't disappointed. It was everything I thought it would be, a junkyard. The Murray River flowed past near the house, hence the reason it was on stilts. There were old cars and boats and all kinds of things in various states of repair lying about. We climbed some old wooden stairs up to the house and went inside. It was dark despite the sun outside, and in an instant, a small dog came at me and began humping my leg with the rhythm of a machine gun. I tried to kick it off, but it was holding on tight and wouldn't let go. It must have finally got what it wanted because it rolled off panting and lay on its back and went to sleep.

As my eyes adjusted to the darkness Croc Man introduced us to his wife and two sons. We were still very much in hill billy country by the look of them. They looked at us like we had just asked where the bath was. I was frantic to get back to Adelaide I knew I couldn't stay here. By now I was desperate for the toilet.

"Can I use the toilet?" I asked Croc Man's wife.

She pointed to a small toilet which was directly off this main room where everyone was sat. I walked into the room and turned to close the door as they were all watching me. There was no door on the toilet!

"Oh, fuck no," I thought. "Where's the door?" I asked.

"Aint one," came the reply.

"Oh, okay," I replied, pretending to laugh.

I tried to pee, but I could feel their eyes burning into me, and I couldn't get started. Then I heard sniggering. I forced myself to the point I thought my bladder would explode. And eventually a trickle started, but I couldn't maintain it, so I pretended I had finished.

"Is that it?" they mocked.

"Yeh small bladder," I grinned back.

Croc Man showed us around his land, but my mind was on how to get back to Adelaide. In the end, I concocted a story that I needed to get back so I could get back to the UK fast as there was a problem at home. I felt guilty, but I really couldn't have stayed in Croc Man's yard for two weeks. I did get back to Adelaide and that night one of the senior fire officers invited me to dinner in a normal house.

When the actual challenge arrived a month or so later, we flew back down

I was assigned to all the organisation side and driving the truck. After a clash of personalities with the same lad who took us to the Hill Billy's house on the first trip, despite it being my challenge, primarily my hard work in getting sponsorship and free flights from Singapore airlines I decided to leave. So, I caught a flight back to Singapore and then on to the UK. This team member had a reputation for being awkward and despite my protests organised for us to stay once again in the shack in the outback and not in the comfort of the fire station in Adelaide, where I needed to be for the radio and TV interviews. All credit to the three they went on to complete it.

Following this again with a friend we organised for several Israeli surgeons to cycle from the Golan Heights to the Schneider Children's Medical Centre of Israel in Petach Tikvah. Again, I was in the administration role due to my ongoing knee problems. I again secured free flights and accommodation.

We stayed for the first night in a place called Netanya. Netanya is a city in the Northern Central District of Israel and is the capital of the surrounding Sharon Plain, 18 miles north of Tel Aviv. We stayed in a roof top luxury apartment of a wonderful couple. One of whom was a doctor with the World Health Organisation. The apartment overlooked the Mediterranean Sea, and I took full advantage of swimming each day.

It was a superb event and raised money for both a children's hospice back here in the UK and the Schneider Children's Medical Centre of Israel, which treats all children regardless of race or creed. I was privileged enough to watch a baby undergoing a heart operation. As we drove through Israel in a support vehicle, I was lucky enough to see just how beautiful Israel is from the Crusader forts to the Sea of Galilee and the stunning biblical Jerusalem. I marvelled at the sight of Nazareth which I had sung about in school as a child and watched in all the big films on a Sunday as a child.

At the end, all the cyclists received a fantastic reception and were greeted by the media and TV stations. I was asked to get up and address the crowd which I did. I did feel proud that this was my idea and I had pulled it off. Not missing the opportunity for a bit of nepotism, on this event I had taken my brother in law, John, with me and when I had finished talking, knowing how shy he was regarding public speaking, I invited him up to say a few words. As he looked towards the podium, I could see a mixture of horror and desperation on his face, as he digested I had just set him up in the most spectacular way ever. He went from a deceased white to a tomato red and he walked towards the podium like a man going to the gallows. He said less than a few words and staggered back to his seat and glanced at me with what can only be described as 'you are dead' kind of look on his face. I was actually a little concerned, but I couldn't stop laughing for me timing was everything, and I got him. It was the icing on the cake.

I learned the very sad news that my childhood friend, Mick Price, was suffering from cancer. Mick eventually succumbed to it, but by all accounts, he was as I knew he would be courageous and showed courage right to the end. On learning of his untimely death, I was deeply saddened. It seemed so unfair that a man with a young family and still so much to offer should be taken by this dreadful disease that takes old and young indiscriminately. Mick, like my sister, Ally, was only in his early forties.

In 2007, I was given the opportunity to return to the Falkland Islands where I had served as a young 21-year-old soldier on Rapier Anti-aircraft Missile Systems. All of which is in my first book 'Not for Queen and Country'. During my time in the Army, I become lifelong friends with a lad from Cumbria, Tony McNally, 'Mack', who I served with in the Falklands and who was also given a chance to return. When I received the call saying I could go, I felt a mixture of excitement and trepidation.

This was most certainly not a holiday, it was a 'Pilgrimage'. It was my chance to return to those far away Islands where I had seen death and war, and it was forever seared into my mind. I had heard conflicting advice from people on whether to return or not. Some people suggested it was a bad idea and would stir old memories whereas others said it would be good to the place in peace and put old ghosts to rest. Both Mack and I decided to go.

We stayed in the Union Jack Club in London, an Armed Forces club hotel. Margaret Thatcher, the former Prime Minister, who took the decision in 1982 to send us to war, came to see us off the night before. As I stood there, she walked past and suddenly grabbed my hand as if to shake it. At that moment, someone asked her a question, and she turned to answer it. I began to pull my hand away, but her grip became full, and she held on tight to my hand.

I was stood there for a minute or two holding her hand, and then she turned and said, "Thank you," and then she was gone.

Just over two hundred veterans were on the pilgrimage, and we flew out from Gatwick airport stopping over in Rio de Janeiro, Brazil, and then down South America on to the Falkland Islands. The tension on the aircraft was palpable. Here was a whole bunch of men who had seen death and destruction, lost friends and had their lives altered, with both physical and mental injuries, about to return to the scene of the crime.

As we approached Falkland's airspace a Royal Air Force Typhoon fighter jet came up on our starboard side, and in response, some of the veterans dropped their trousers to show their contempt for the RAF in a friendly gesture. The pilot gave the two fingers and dropped off into the blue yonder. I looked out the window and caught my first glimpse of the Islands and felt the emotion rise in me. We landed at RAF Mount Pleasant and received a warm welcome. There were signs saying, 'Welcome back lads' which was a better reception than we received from the occupying Argentine troops all those years earlier.

We boarded a small coach which took us to the barracks in Port Stanley where Mack and I were staying. Some of the veterans had elected to stay in the homes of the local population, but I preferred to stay in the barracks. It was to be a weeklong visit, and during that week there were several receptions and parades organised, but I decided I didn't want to get involved in the public side of it. I was here to see where I had fought and pay my respects to the lads who never came back.

We had our first walk into Port Stanley, and the change was very dramatic from our last sight of it. When we had got into Stanley, the place was utter chaos. Some buildings were still burning, dead bodies lying about and many thousands of Argentine soldiers. Now normality was back, and there were shops and restaurants and such. I couldn't help noticing the youths who walked about and thinking that they were not even born when we liberated their home town. There was still a pub, The Globe Hotel, which had weapons and guns from the war hanging on the wall. I found it rather distasteful myself and felt the place would have been better with a total refit, perhaps a tasteful painting showing a scene from our war but it looked scruffy and very worn and tired, possibly I was missing the point?

A few days into our visit Mack and I hired a jeep and set off for San Carlos, the place we had landed under enemy air attack all those years before. It is about 50 miles or so and while there is a road for some of the way it soon turns to rough track and then grass and hills. It was pleasant looking at the vistas as we made our way to San Carlos. I was looking at it with older and wiser eyes this time and as a civilian and not a soldier. Mack and I laughed and joked as we drove but underneath this bravado lay a real fear at seeing the place we fought at.

After leaving any semblance of a road, we drove through mud and large flooded puddles that looked like small lakes and through farms until we eventually caught sight of San Carlos. We stopped the jeep and got out. As we were higher up, it gave us a stunning view of it.

"Well mate there it is," Mack said.

"Yeah, after all these years were back" I replied, hardly believing it.

San Carlos was bathed in bright sunshine and looked the picture of beauty. It was hard to think that it was once the scene of such vicious fighting. We drove down into the settlement and received a warm reception from the owners who welcomed us with a well-needed cup of tea and cakes. The couple were actually in the UK during the invasion and so were lucky enough to have missed it. They gently probed Mack and I about our role during the war, and we told them bits.

It was lambing season at the time and Mack, and I helped round-up a couple of the little babies up. After more tea, we decided we would go and find my trench and the site of our Rapier during the war. It had been a long time, but I was still pretty confident that I could find it.

We walked across the tussock grass which I found hard with my bad knees but after stopping and looking about we walked right on to our old position. I was totally amazed to find the place was still there. The trenches had collapsed, but it was still there where we had dug the Rapier in. The debris of war still lay about, like barbed wire, old camouflage netting, metal poles and such. I sat down now feeling very emotional and very sad.

I looked at the water of San Carlos before me and saw the floating buoy marking the spot where HMS Antelope had been hit and sunk two nights after we had landed. The blast had blinded me and knocked me on my arse. I remembered the Argentine Jets screaming in dropping their bombs and strafing with the large calibre machine guns. Mack said he was going to walk back to the farm to give me time to sit and reflect.

I sat alone and began to gently sob. I'm not sure why but I felt an overwhelming sense of guilt that I had survived and many had not. Many of the people I loved and thought about when I had sat here fighting during that war were now gone, and I had a wife and two children who were my priority. How the years change. With a whoosh and a roar an RAF Typhoon jet swept over me, and for a second I was back in the fight. Like an idiot, I waved and then realised how stupid I was. However, he turned back and flew back over dipping his wings. I stood up and said a prayer and took one last look and walked away. This place had taken up enough of my life, and now I would leave it.

Mack and I drove to Bluff Cove the place where the troop ship, Sir Galahad, had been hit, killing nearly 50 men, mostly of the Welsh Guards. Mack had been operating the Rapier when that attacks came in, but a technical fault had prevented him shooting down the lead attacking aircraft, which has had a significant effect on him and still does to this day. He did, however, manage to shoot down a Skyhawk that was following the attacks to survey the damage. The full story of his war can be read in the superb and very emotional book he has written called 'Still watching men burn'.

The week over we boarded the plane for the arduous 24-hour journey back to the UK. Did the pilgrimage help me or indeed Mack overcome and lay some of our ghosts to rest? The answer is no, I know Mack suffered major problems on his return and as for me, it had raked over old memories some I had even put to the back of my mind. It had reawakened the traumas I had felt on my initial return. I know it works for some people but for me, and certainly for Mack equally, it was a mistake to return.

In 2012 both my daughter, Kristy, and son, Nathan, married within a short time of each other. Nathan, in the beautiful and historic Roman City of Chester, to Jenny, a sweet and generous woman. Then shortly after Kristy to Adam, a Doctor of Chemistry, a decent and generous man, in the church of Bishopric (Episkopi) on the beautiful Greek Island of Skopelos.

About a year after returning from Kristy and Adam's wedding, in Greece, I felt like a sensation of dry skin on my right leg. It felt rough, and it tingled if I brushed against anything even a smooth bedsheet. I was at the doctors for an injection in my knee and mentioned it to her. She checked it over and prescribed a moisturiser which I applied for a week or two. It made no difference, and the sensation began to spread down my leg on my lower back and buttocks. It also took on a feeling of pins and needles. I had various blood tests and such, but it got worse and worse spreading up my back. The only distraction was that Kristy was now pregnant with her first child and our first grandchild. A private scan revealed that she was having a little boy and he would be called Henry.

I was pottering in the garden in the last of the warm weather in November 2014, about a week before Kristy was due to give birth to Henry on or about November 5th. I felt a little unwell, and my throat was a little sore, but I put it down to a cold and Tricia declared I had man flu! I had a bath and got into the spare bed as I had begun to get hot and cold shivers.

Later that night I had a raging sore throat, and I decided to drag myself up to the out of hours doctor at the local hospital. He said I had a severe throat infection and prescribed some antibiotics. I went home and took them. I remember little of the next hours apart from the fact I had no idea where I was or any concept of events. I was hallucinating, shivering and sweating.

Tricia rang the hospital who advised putting me in a taxi. She explained that it would not be possible due to how ill I was. They said if possible they would send an on-call doctor out but couldn't guarantee it. I don't remember any of this, but apparently, a doctor did come out and took one look at me and rang for an ambulance. I was taken to hospital where I was found to be suffering from Pneumonia and swelling on the brain. I was taken to an isolation room and put on drips, and there I lay in and out of it totally unaware of my surroundings apart from the odd, weird dream or hallucination.

They battled with various antiviral drugs to stabilise me and bring my dangerously high temperature down. In the middle of this chaos, Kristy was over the other side of the hospital, in the maternity section, where on the 5th November she gave birth to Henry. I was out of it. Tricia was running between the buildings, and it must have been a very exhausting time for her

As I began to recover I was informed my white blood cells were low. At one point a consultant with a very abrupt attitude came into my room and asked me if I had ever had an HIV test as men of my age should not be getting Pneumonia. No, I replied taken aback, but I will have one if you want. I did and as I knew it was negative. I began to eat again only small bits at first but my strength was slowly returning, and I could walk up and down the corridor of the hospital. Finally, I was well enough to go home, and at last, I would meet my grandson Henry.

I got home and took it very easy due to lack of strength but my mood was boosted when Kristy and Adam arrived with Henry, and I finally got to hold him. It was a moment I will never forget, and I loved him unconditionally in an instant.

My symptoms continued as far as the tingling on my skin was concerned, but I also began to feel what I can only describe as unwell. I couldn't put my finger on it, but something wasn't right. After seeing many specialists, my doctor said he thought it was all probably down to my Post Battle Stress Disorder. I disagreed, and so did my psychologist who I had been seeing a lot of years, Doctor Peter Higson. Strangely enough, my blood tests were coming back with low white blood cells, but I was repeatedly told this had nothing to do with it. I was at my wit's end to get them to, believe me, it wasn't in my mind but my pleas fell on deaf ears, and I considered at one point they might be right.

In May of 2016, my older brother Peter's health began to fail. He had suffered from diabetes for many years, but a fall at home put him into the hospital. After falling at home, he spent a long time lying on the floor waiting for an ambulance as apparently it wasn't classed as urgent and there were no ambulances available in the area. My brother was eventually taken to a hospital, where his treatment or lack of it is now a legal dispute, but whatever, he suffered, and his condition deteriorated, and his organs began to shut down. I could talk with him while he was still conscious and we spoke of life and of his imminent death. I asked if he was scared and he said firmly, "No," he was facing it not with courage but with a calm and collected acceptance that this is the end and we all have an end. My brother died, and another chapter of my life closed. I will admire him forever.

After more blood tests, and a few days later I went back to my Doctors where I saw a doctor who has a liking for homoeopathic medicine. He sat there looking like he had just come off a protest to save some trees in a blend of scruffy wild coloured and worn out clothes with a jumper full of holes and wild, unkempt hair Leo Sayer would have been proud of at his peak.

"I've come about the blood test results," I opened.

"Yeh," he replied, "what shall we do?"

"I really don't know," I answered truthfully.

"Well let's keep an eye on them," he said and then advised I should begin to reduce my medication for other conditions.

Ok, I thought then, you're the doctor I will go along with what you say. However, a few days later I received a letter to go and see a Haematology consultant at the hospital.

The day arrived, and Tricia and I went along. We tried to book in, but someone approached us and told us we needed to go upstairs to the Haematology ward. I was really puzzled now as in all the times I had been for blood tests it had been in the clinic. We booked in and sat down, and I was glancing about, and then I looked down at the table where there were numerous magazines on cars and boats etc. However, there were also magazines with CANCER and MYELOMA written on them. I didn't know what Myeloma was, but I knew what cancer meant!

We were called into the consultant's office, and he began explaining that there were indicators present in my blood that may indicate a form of blood cancer and that I would have to have a bone marrow biopsy! In the space of twenty minutes, I had gone from thinking I was having a blood test to talking about bone marrow and possibly having cancer! I stayed calm because incredibly I felt calm. We left the office in a bit of a daze, but my only concern was Tricia.

The following Monday I underwent the bone marrow biopsy and then had to wait just a week for the results. Tricia was out when the phone went, and it was a nurse from the Haematology unit. The tests were inconclusive she informed me. They hadn't found anything.

"We will have to do the test again," she told me, "only deeper."

"Okay," I said I really had no option, but at least the first one was negative.

I had the painful biopsy again waited nearly two weeks for my appointment. Once again Tricia and I went to the Haematology unit, and after a small wait, we were called the consultant's offices.

"Well," he said, "I'm afraid the tests have revealed you have Multi Myeloma, a form of blood cancer."

He went on to explain that it was not curable but could be managed. It will shorten your life he said. I remained calm, and I accepted my fate there and then. I didn't and never will feel sorry for myself it is life, and you get what you get. My only concern was and will be for Tricia, my daughter, son and grandchildren. I don't know how long I will live, but no one does. So, make the most of what you have and don't worry about what you haven't.

What does life hold for me now? Where do I go from here? Well, the simple truth is I don't know, but neither does anyone else. The real truth is the moment we are born we are walking towards the gallows, and nothing will ever interrupt that journey because the destination is inevitable. However, what we do on that walk is in our hands, and it will ultimately make a difference at the end as to what you did in life.

I have no real regrets because it makes no difference anyway. Am I sorry for some of my actions? Yes, I am, and with hindsight, I might have done some things differently but what's done is done. Whatever wealth and material things you have gathered in your life from your house to your car and prized possessions at the end they mean nothing and will end up in someone else's hands one day. We are the custodians of everything we have, but that is it, nothing is ours to keep; we leave this world as we came in empty handed. What really matters is who we loved and who loved us. That is the real achievement of any person, and that is the true purpose of being here.

I have learned that there are people who will hate you no matter what you do, and that is a fact of life, but if you refuse to hate those people back then it leaves them with the hate in their own heart alone and not yours. If you want to be truly happy then I think the real secret is to make other people happy and do what you can to better other people's lives rather than just your own and it will enrich your own life even more than theirs, and you will both be better people.

I hope you enjoyed my journey, but I hope you enjoy your own much more.

Edward Denmark 2016

NOT FOR QUEEN AND COUNTRY

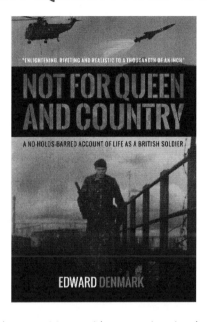

From Army cadets on Merseyside to action in the Falklands and Northern Ireland Edward Denmark joined the British army for adventure, and to serve Queen and country. However, as he prepared to go ashore in the frozen, windswept Falkland Islands 8000 miles from Britain, facing a well dug in, larger enemy force, he understood at that moment that this was not for Queen and Country. He was now fighting for his own life, and the chance to see the sunrise once more. Follow this young soldier as he endures the bitter cold and constant air attack by a very determined Argentine enemy in the Falklands war, to patrolling the brutally violent streets of Northern Ireland, where tragedy came from nowhere. If you have ever wondered what our soldiers face in war and how they keep going under the most arduous and desperate conditions, then this book will tell you.

Printed in Great Britain
by Amazon